GAME OF MY LIFE

RAMS

Horns Up!

Jay Paris

GAME OF MY LIFE

RAMS

MEMORABLE STORIES OF RAMS FOOTBALL

BY JAY PARIS

FOREWORD BY DICK ENBERG

SPORTS PUBLISHING

Sports Publishing books may be purchased in bulk at special discounts for sales promotion, corporate gifts, fund-raising, or educational purposes. Special editions can also be created to specifications. For details, contact the Special Sales Department, Sports Publishing, 307 West 36th Street, 11th Floor, New York, NY 10018 or sportspubbooks@skyhorsepublishing.com.

Sports Publishing® is a registered trademark of Skyhorse Publishing, Inc.®, a Delaware corporation.

Visit our website at www.sportspubbooks.com.

10 9 8 7 6 5 4 3 2 1

Library of Congress Cataloging-in-Publication Data is available on file.

Interior photos courtesy of the Rams, unless otherwise noted.

Cover design by Tom Lau
Cover photo courtesy of Roman Gabriel

ISBN: 978-1-68358-105-5
Ebook ISBN: 978-1-68358-106-2
Printed in the United States of America

CONTENTS

ACKNOWLEDGMENTS

This book underscores my lifelong love affair with the Rams. That connection was nurtured by three people who deserve to be acknowledged for their contributions.

Frank King, or Uncle Frank to me, was a huge Los Angeles Rams fan. He introduced me to the Rams and their great heritage. Fall Sundays were special because of him and his passion for the Rams.

Jack McKinney, a friend and former college player, taught me how to watch the Rams. Instead of focusing on the football, he suggested to observe the blocking and other nuances. His top-deck, front-row seats at Anaheim Stadium were always a keen perch from which to learn the finer points of the game.

Eric Sense, another colleague, had a zest for the Rams, and life, which matched mine. Any contest at any location against any team and Sense was all-in, eager to join me for another serving of Rams football.

Julie Ganz, my editor, also deserves praises for putting all these words in the appropriate order. This project isn't completed minus her unselfish work.

Lastly, my wife Julie, and our sons Conor and Phil, are the foundation for my career, which has included covering the NFL for nearly three decades. Football is the ultimate team sport, and that goes for those writing about it as well. My teammates, in my eyes, made all this possible.

—Jay Paris

FOREWORD

By Dick Enberg

When turning the pages of *Game of My Life Rams*, I'm reminded of the amazing memories this grand franchise has produced. Some of the recollections came during my enjoyable stint of calling the team's games, from 1966 to 1977, as an announcer for Gene Autry's KMPC radio station.

What's clear are the thrills, chills, and, yes, heartache, which Rams fans have often consumed. When those games were played in the historic Los Angeles Memorial Coliseum, with more than 100,000 fans cheering, it only amplified what a special time it was in Southern California's rich sports history.

What's keen about the book is that the players selected which game they wanted highlighted. Their reasons for picking the game of their life were as varied as the players themselves.

From quarterback Jim Hardy trying to steal snaps from Bob Waterfield on the first Los Angeles Rams team in 1946 to Pro Bowl kicker Johnny Hekker booting the current squad out of poor field position.

From Roman Gabriel winning in consecutive weeks against Bart Starr and Johnny Unitas in 1967 to Gabriel's trusty tight end, Billy Truax, making another clutch catch.

From Fred Dryer—who would later be known as "Hunter" to a generation of TV viewers—getting a kick out of Gabriel's misfortune to Tom Mack breaking in a rookie named Dennis Harrah by unmercifully calling him "Bird Legs."

And for the record, I will confirm that Mack did not move on that bogus illegal procedure call in the loss to the Vikings in the 1974 NFC Championship Game!

There's Rod Perry illustrating how class shows no matter what the score, when he tells how close he came to knocking away Terry Bradshaw's touchdown pass to John Stallworth, which turned the tide in the Steelers' favor in Super Bowl XIV at the Rose Bowl.

Just maybe if Stallworth didn't produce a catch for the ages over a leaping Perry, the Rams would have prevailed for their only Super Bowl title with Los Angeles in front of their name.

Jack Youngblood, a.k.a. Capt. Blood, speaks of playing in that Super Bowl with a broken leg. What I had forgotten is that he suited up for the Pro Bowl as well. Youngblood was often called the John Wayne of the NFL, and it's easy to see why.

Which reminds me of the story told here of Gabriel sharing the big screen with the Duke in *The Undefeated*.

With their proximity to Hollywood, it seems one Ram or another was often reading cue cards. But no one had to yell "action" when Harrah and others took off to pummel the Jets' Mark Gastineau after he broke into his sack dance at Shea Stadium. That caused a rumble that still stands among the most spirited in NFL history.

How about LeRoy Irvin bringing back two punts for touchdowns in one game! Or Mike Lansford's game-winning kick against the Saints to cap an unlikely comeback.

And we can't forget a high-stepping Eric Dickerson and a hard-hitting Kevin Greene, two Hall of Famers who created havoc on both sides of the ball.

I would be remiss in rewinding my Rams time machine and not mentioning my dear friend, Merlin Olsen. Not only did I have the pleasure of calling the 14-time Pro Bowler's games, but he was later by my side in the NBC broadcasting booth, always eager to help our network team. Olsen, a TV star in the series *Father Murphy*, was a star in the booth, as well. An Academic All-America player, he generously shared his keen football knowledge with everyone on the broadcast team.

Considering his unselfish work with the Rams, that comes as little surprise.

What's shocking is all these memories belong to one franchise and they've been collected in one book. Jay Paris, a longtime, award-winning NFL sportswriter, has brought these stories, and more, to life.

One can almost see the Los Angeles Memorial Coliseum's cauldron flickering in the distance. Or hear the roar of the L.A. crowd yelling "Charge!" as a big play is delivered by their football hero wearing horns on his helmet.

When reflecting on the unpredictable Rams, the excitement they have produced, and the compelling tales in this book, there are only two words that come to mind: "Oh My!"

So settle in and enjoy your journey into the Rams' storied history, all presented here by one of our finest writers.

—Dick Enberg

INTRODUCTION

The Rams in Los Angeles just sounds right.

We know about their history in St. Louis and Cleveland, and no offense to those fine municipalities. That's where the Rams called "home" when winning the Super Bowl in 2000 and the NFL title in 1945, respectively.

But with the Rams returning to the City of Angels, it seems the L.A. sports world has welcomed back a familiar friend.

The Rams planted their flag in L.A. in 1946, bringing the world of professional sports to an area that has embraced that form of entertainment from the get-go like few others.

Going to a Rams game was as much of an event as it was about final score. Hollywood stars were in the stands and when many Rams weren't on the field, they were waiting for a director to supply their cue.

Both the silver screens and TV screens ached for Rams to fill roles, in everything from *The Undefeated* to *Gilligan's Island*. It reinforced the players' standing in the community and just how important it was to be a Ram, or a Rams fan.

Long before the Dodgers crowed about "Dodger Blue" or the Lakers introduced a West Virginia shooting guard with a crew cut named Jerry West, the Rams were the sports foundation in this area known for its shaky ground.

Sure, the earth shook when the Rams relocated from L.A. to Anaheim in 1980, and there was a tsunami of angst when they exited Anaheim for St. Louis in 1995.

But all that is in the memory bank, and it doesn't diminish the snapshots of Rams moments that any booster holds dear: a pinpoint Roman Gabriel pass to Billy Truax's reliable hands, the Fearsome Foursome pulverizing another petrified quarterback, and Tom Mack's dominant blocking for 13 seasons, a span in which the Rams had 12 winning years.

If you squint, one can imagine animated coach George Allen, in his well-creased, short-sleeved white shirt and ramrod straight tie, roaming the sidelines making sure everyone knew the future really was now.

There's Jack Youngblood mauling an overmatched offensive lineman, Eric Dickerson high-stepping toward another end zone, or Henry Ellard springing high in the air to snag a Jim Everett attempt.

Those recollections come rushing back, many with the historic Los Angeles Memorial Coliseum in the forefront. With the Olympic cauldron flickering and the snow-capped San Gabriel Mountains providing a backdrop to the L.A. skyscrapers, the Coliseum rocked with crowds approaching 100,000.

Those Rams patrons will soon be heading to a state-of-the-art facility in nearby Inglewood. The Rams are charging into a new era, but that doesn't erase what this grand team has done and the good times it's produced.

When growing up in Southern California, I fell hard for that cool helmet with the horns on it—thank you Frank Gehrke, a former Rams running back who painted the first one in 1948. And I was just like every other kid on my block.

On game days my uncle, a proud and tough marine, would gather his kids, myself, and my buddies and we would pile into his car for fall excursions to L.A.'s Exposition Park.

Back then, a military member in uniform was charged 50 cents for a ticket and he could bring in six young 'uns with him for free. On many Sundays, I got to be one of those tykes tagging along.

When approaching the iconic venue, the Coliseum always stood out. It was bigger than life to a youngster, as it dominated the landscape off Figueroa Street, which was also set aside for museums, rose gardens, and later, the L.A. Sports Arena.

But none of those things clogged the vision of a lucky kid getting to go cheer his favorite team. And if I did so while wearing my battered, single-bar Rams youth helmet, all the better.

The Rams are back, and like many, I can't wait to see where they are headed. But they set course into the future with a treasure trove of memories, many of which are rekindled in the following pages.

Chapter 1

JIM HARDY

Rams at Lions—October 24, 1948

BIRTH DATE:	April 4, 1923
HOMETOWN:	Los Angeles
RESIDENCE:	La Quinta, California
JERSEY NO.:	21
POSITION:	Quarterback
HEIGHT:	6 feet
WEIGHT:	180 pounds

The Run-Up

Jim Hardy was a terrific University of Southern California quarterback, leading it to consecutive Rose Bowl victories in 1944–45.

What made those triumphs even sweeter was both times Hardy beat USC's archrival, UCLA, to reach Pasadena. And in the first year, that meant a win over the team led by the Bruins' fabulous quarterback Bob Waterfield.

The two players and their schools were fierce competitors in an era when college football ruled the Southern California sports landscape. The Rams had yet to arrive from Cleveland, let alone the Dodgers from Brooklyn or the Lakers from Minneapolis.

While the Rams had yet to forge their L.A. history before arriving in 1946, the same couldn't be said about Hardy and Waterfield.

Or is it Hatfield and McCoy?

"Although Bob was a great guy, we didn't get along," Hardy said. "We had a clash of personalities."

The two were intense competitors, and that same script rang true in the NFL. Waterfield got a head start on his pro career before Hardy finished his navy stint.

"Waterfield got out of the army the year before because he had a bad knee," Hardy said. "He went back to being a civilian and then playing for the Cleveland Rams in 1945. He was the MVP his rookie season and they won the championship."

While Waterfield was being a star, Hardy was a shining light with his brother, Don, on the USS Maryland. The battleship saw considerable action in World War II in the Pacific Theater.

Once the war ended, the friction between Hardy and Waterfield, the former BMOCs on the respective L.A. campuses, began its second act.

Hardy was selected by the Washington Redskins in the first round, but quickly made an audible he's long regretted.

"Dumbest thing I ever did," he said.

Instead of going to Washington, Hardy requested a trade in 1946. That was the same year the newfangled Rams planted their flag in L.A.

"When I came back home when the war was over I had been gone for over a year," Hardy said. "We had just had our first son [James]. I decided I didn't want to go away from home anymore."

When word leaked about Hardy's trepidation of leaving, Redskins owner George Marshall delivered some inside information.

"Listen, the Rams are going to move from Cleveland," Marshall told Hardy. "I will work something out so you can sign with the Rams."

Hardy was ecstatic about staying, but not eager about the name above him on the Rams' depth chart: Bob Waterfield.

"Like a dummy I signed with the Rams after Waterfield had played well and led the Rams to the championship," Hardy said. "I couldn't get into a ball game for two years. Oh, I would play once in a while but I wanted to go somewhere where I could start."

Those two L.A. gunslingers who had been crosstown rivals were in the crosshairs again. A patient Hardy, an ex-Pacific Coast Conference MVP, waited until his third season with the Rams before the game of his life.

"I couldn't get a break as for two years Waterfield kept my butt on the bench," Hardy said. "That was difficult to take. Because we beat that UCLA team with Waterfield and Don Paul, for the Pacific Coast Conference title and the chance to go to the Rose Bowl."

While Waterfield's career bloomed, Hardy's had trouble taking root.

"I had to sit behind Waterfield," Hardy said, "and it galled me something terrible."

The Game

By Jim Hardy

After my second year I called [owner] Dan Reeves and told him that I didn't want to come back to the Rams. I wanted to play and I wasn't doing that much behind [Bob] Waterfield.

But we had hired a new coach, Clark Shaughnessy, and Dan told me why don't you talk to him first. So I went out to his home in the Santa Monica area. He told me that whoever is playing the best football will start.

That was all I wanted was an even chance. And he lived up to it.

Bob would start some games and if he went sour, then they would put me in. And it was like that the other way around, too. It was like being a pitcher and if you were hot, you stayed in there. If not, [Shaughnessy] would take you out and put in the other guy.

We would alternate and each of us started half the games. We each threw 14 touchdown passes, but Bob had [11] more interceptions than I did [in 1948].

He started in this game in Detroit and we were favored to beat the Lions. But they had us down in the third quarter, 21–0. I'm sitting my butt on the bench next to the water cooler.

Bob wasn't doing anything so Shaughnessy comes over to me and says you're going in. From there we scored five times and won the game, 34–27.

Playing with the Rams I had some good days and some not-so-good-days. But coming from behind and getting hot to win that game was my highlight of playing with the Rams.

I threw two touchdown passes, both to Tom Keane [his only two scores of the season].

And I went a lot to Red Hickey. He was our starting left end and he was just a great receiver. He also was a basketball guy; he was a big guy and had fabulous moves.

He would come back into the huddle and say, "Jim, I'm good on this and I'm good on that." And when he said that I knew that was like running down and putting money in the back.

He could fake and catch—he was good.

I threw a lot of passes to him that day so after the game we went out to dinner in downtown Detroit.

And I still remember what a thrill that day was and how much fun it was to bring the team back to the victory.

There are two couples in the booth next to us and it was clear they had been drinking. Detroit was dry on Sunday and you couldn't get any booze but these people got it somewhere.

They start carrying on with each other and pretty soon there's an altercation and it got scary.

Hickey was tougher than nails, and a big guy, and he just flies right into the middle of this thing.

Me? I head for the kitchen, find the alley, and I'm gone.

I see Hickey the next morning and he comes up to me with this big lump over one eye and he looked really bad.

Hickey said, "What happened to you?"

Look I didn't know who the hell these people were. I wasn't going to get killed getting involved so I got the hell out of

Hardy was a player who stayed at home after finishing college. A star in the Los Angeles Memorial Coliseum while at USC, Hardy's battles with teammate Bob Waterfield, an ex-UCLA standout, for the starting role extended their crosstown rivalry to another level. (AP Photo)

there and went back to the Cadillac Hotel, where we were staying two blocks away.

So the game of my life had two stories to it.

But in a nutshell, that game was the highlight of my Rams career. I was the player of the game and I still have the game ball.

Then that night after the game with Hickey is one I will never forget.

The Aftermath

There's seven days in a week. And on a majority of them, the 94-year-old Jim Hardy is training at the gym.

"I feel pretty good," Hardy said. "I don't have any permanent problems."

Hardy keeps plugging away, just like he did when backing up Bob Waterfield. If not for Hardy's perseverance, it's possible Hardy would have never brought the Rams back in his memorable game at Detroit in 1948.

Maybe the attitude comes from Hardy's devotion to his beloved alma mater, USC. Its motto is "Fight On," and is there any former Trojan who's a better example of doing just that than Hardy?

The scrappy quarterback who led USC to consecutive Rose Bowl titles is still a fixture with the program.

Despite USC's downtown L.A. campus being some 130 miles away from Hardy's Palm Springs-area home, he attends practice once a week.

"I've been in good stead with the coaches and athletic directors there forever," Hardy said, as he rattled off their names with precision and admiration.

Hardy's list goes back a ways and illustrates his prideful connection to USC. It's a bond that started when Hardy was a tyke and his father, Russell, worked for Western Union.

When the elder Hardy was sending dispatches of college games, his football-loving sons were usually at his side.

"I was eight years old and my dad did the telegraph for Western Union and worked the press bowl for the USC and UCLA games," Hardy said. "He would take the stories from the sportswriters and with his telegraph key send them out to the eastern news outlets.

"Me and my brother went to the last game in 1931 and the Trojans beat Georgia, 60–0. I fell in love with the Trojans that day.

"When I was growing up I had all their pictures all over my walls. I wanted to go to USC in the worst way. I couldn't wait to get older and play for USC."

It seems inconceivable the Rose Bowl could be played minus Hardy's presence. He went to the game to cap that 1931 season and he's been to every one in Pasadena since.

It's believed to be the longest streak by anyone attending the Rose Bowl.

Hardy did miss the Rose Bowl in 1942, when it was moved to North Carolina during World War II because of national security reasons.

Otherwise, the kid who knelt each night and repeated the same prayer, "Please make me a USC football player," is nearly as big a part of the Rose Bowl tradition as the parade down Colorado Boulevard.

He's been to 85 straight contests, which are known as the Granddaddy of the bowl games. It'll surprise few people if Hardy makes No. 86 next New Year's Day.

Chapter 2

ROMAN GABRIEL

Packers at Rams—December 9, 1967
Colts at Rams—December 17, 1967

BIRTH DATE:	August 5, 1940
HOMETOWN:	Wilmington, North Carolina
RESIDENCE:	Charlotte, North Carolina
JERSEY NO.:	18
POSITION:	Quarterback
HEIGHT:	6 foot 5
WEIGHT:	220 pounds

The Run-Up

The reason Roman Gabriel would go on to win the NFL MVP award in 1969 and ultimately have his game of his life was because of one George Herbert Allen.

The coach known for his motto of "the future is now" took a flyer on an unproven Gabriel.

It was a smart move by a smart coach. Or was he really that keen?

"I remember once we went to play in Green Bay and it must have been 30 below zero," Gabriel said.

Allen wasn't fazed.

"This is Rams weather!" he told his chattering collection of players.

Gabriel rolled his eyes and reached for another jacket.

"I was an Academic All-American at North Carolina State," Gabriel said. "I know the difference between cold and warm, and this was not Rams weather at all."

But Allen was all-in on Gabriel. And the feeling was mutual.

"He was a players' coach, and looking back on it, he never had a losing record," Gabriel said. "He never looked at a team as having problems. Instead they were challenges waiting to be solved.

Gabriel was well-versed in cooling his jets. He had done just that in anticipating his own opportunity as a starting quarterback. When Allen replaced Harland Svare in 1966, Gabriel's ascent to stardom received a turbo-sized boost.

"I hadn't had a chance before that," Gabriel said.

He did make the most of becoming friends with Rosey Grier, the team's defensive stalwart.

"Rosey was always such a real leader," Gabriel said.

Even if he pursued hobbies that most football players didn't—off the field.

"I remember my rookie year [1962] I was walking through the locker room and I went by Rosey," Gabriel said. "At that time he was a little bit bigger than 320 pounds and he was sitting there needle pointing. I just remember that and how he called me over to him and he introduced himself.

"The whole time that I knew Rosey when we were playing he was always very cordial and he is still one of the best guys that I know."

But did the Rams realize what they had in Gabriel? Not really.

In his first four years Gabriel started just 23 games.

"We went 11-11-1," Gabriel said. "The quarterbacks that started the other games over that time were 4-27-2."

Allen changed all that. He told Gabriel at the onset that he would be the No. 1 quarterback, based on what Allen saw him do as the No. 2 quarterback.

"We had played the Bears when George was a coach there," Gabriel said. "They were beating us pretty bad so I had a chance to play a little in the second half. We lost, but I ended up throwing for 300 yards. George never forgot that and when he came to Los Angeles he told me I had a chance to be a winning quarterback."

Trouble was the Oakland Raiders of the rival AFL held Gabriel in a similar regard. They showed their faith with a stack of money to entice Gabriel to head north.

"I was making $25,000 and they came to Raleigh and offered me $100,000 to switch leagues," Gabriel said.

Once news of the Raiders' offer reached Allen, he reached out to Gabriel.

"You don't want to leave," Allen countered. "If you go to them you could sit on the bench. Trust me, here I will make you the starter."

The Rams upped their compensation for Gabriel, who ended up staying put.

"The NFL was established and the AFL was not," Gabriel said.

And Allen did not go back on his word. Gabriel was inserted as a starter and three years later he was named the NFL's Most Valuable Player.

"I got to prove what Allen thought of me was right," Gabriel said.

"He was such a great coach; remember the Rams hadn't had a winning season since 1958 before he showed up. All he asked of you was that you respect what he did. You didn't have to like him, you just had to respect him.

"He would go to bat for you and he knew every player's family and their names.

"After we started winning, he would have a Monday night get-together and he would play host. He would be engaging and it was a very casual get-together. The more all the players talked on those Monday nights, the more we became friends. We carried it on to Thursday nights and the majority of players would attend. We might have a glass of milk or two."

Gabriel was kidding about the liquid filling the Rams' glasses during their get togethers. But he was certainly not joking when he talked about what Allen meant to him.

"He was a man of his word," said Gabriel, who named a son Ram Allen Gabriel. "I got to play for him for five seasons and those were the best years of my career."

Few Rams were more popular than "Gabe" as he helped return the Rams to being a successful franchise when finally getting his chance as a starter, thanks to coach George Allen. Gabriel was the 1969 NFL MVP as he threw for 24 touchdowns with just seven interceptions.

The final two seasons came only after Gabriel and other Rams stars such as Tom Mack, Dick Bass, and Jack Snow went to bat for Allen after he was fired by owner Dan Reeves following the 1968 season. The players protested, threatening not to play for the Rams if Allen wasn't retained.

That bought the winningest coach in Rams history two more seasons, during one of which Gabriel was selected the MVP.

The Games

By Roman Gabriel

When I think of my game of my life I really think of two. That was at the end of the 1967 season.

We had to beat Green Bay and then Baltimore in the last two games to get into the playoffs.

Baltimore was leading our conference but before we played the Colts we had to beat Green Bay in L.A. We won both games.

During the Green Bay game, the Packers were winning late but the defense held them. With about a minute to go Tony Guillory blocked Donny Anderson's punt. Claude Crabb picked [the football] up and ran it down to the [Packers] 5-yard line.

We didn't have any timeouts so I threw the first pass out of bounds.

Then we called "Pass 46 Power." It ended up being a touchdown pass to Bernie Casey.

We had been running "27 Power and 46 Power." Out of that formation we could run "Pass 46 Power."

So it was a fake run play where we pull the right guard, Joe Scibelli, and we had center Ken Iman and running back Tony

Mason all going left. We made it look like a run as Bernie blocked down into the line; Scibelli had a great block, too.

Bob Jeter, their cornerback, sucked up on the play when he saw the opening. That left Bernie all alone in the end zone. It was an offensive game for us and we won 27–24.

All I had to do was to get him the football and not choke. It's hard sometimes when a guy is that wide open because you have [a] tendency to let off a little bit. That happens if you don't stay with your fundamentals and don't follow through.

So we beat the Packers with Bart Starr and the very next week Baltimore and Johnny Unitas came into L.A. undefeated and we only had one loss, so that was a pretty good matchup. They had two ties and one of them was against us earlier in the year.

If we beat Baltimore, we go to the playoffs. If Baltimore wins, it goes.

But the game wasn't as tight as you would think. We beat them pretty handily, 34–10. It just wasn't a close game.

But those guys got after Johnny Unitas, I think he was sacked seven times that day and Deacon [Jones] forced a fumble.

The Fearsome Foursome, on that day, they couldn't be blocked, I'm telling you.

That was one thing we did that day well and that was control the ball. We got up on them and the defense kept getting them off the field and getting the ball back for us. That's a good way to stop the other team.

There are some games that things go well and that was one of them. I threw three touchdown passes and was 18 of 22. That's a pretty good game—these days, they might throw 22 passes in the first quarter.

I threw an 80-yard touchdown pass to Jack Snow in the second quarter and that put us ahead 10–7. We never trailed after that.

Of course the next week we went to Green Bay for the play-offs even though we had a better record and we had beat them during the season. In those days, it wasn't the team that had the best record that had the home game, it was off of your playoff record the previous year. The Packers were coming off a Super Bowl win so they had the home game.

But when I think back, those two games at the end of the 1967 regular season stand out.

The Aftermath

Roman Gabriel collected his share of awards. From being the NFL's Most Valuable Player in 1969 to its Comeback Player of the Year in 1973, Gabriel's trophy mantle was impressive.

But there's one accolade he never got. To this day, some remind Gabriel of his awesome performance.

"You were great as John Wayne's adopted son," a well-wisher will tell Gabriel. "You should have won the Academy Award."

With the Rams playing at the Los Angeles Memorial Coliseum, that meant the bright lights from movie marquees were just up the Harbor Freeway, which connected with the Hollywood Freeway. While Gabriel revved the Rams' offense, having secured a starting role in 1966, he was also getting movie and TV gigs.

"Being a football player in L.A., you had a chance to meet and work with some great people," Gabriel said.

Gabriel the quarterback wasn't always perfect when a director screamed, "Action!" But Gabriel was part of *The Undefeated* cast, which starred John Wayne.

In an odd occurrence, Gabriel, who was introduced to Wayne by teammate Merlin Olsen, played Wayne's adopted Native American son.

"I do the audition and I get the role," Gabriel said. "Then I had a chance to go to Vietnam to entertain the troops with Bob Hope and John Wayne. What can you say about being around those two?"

But around *The Undefeated* set, certain rules were in place.

"The stunt guys said, 'Look, don't make the mistake of calling Wayne, "Duke,"' Gabriel said. 'He will let you know when you can call him that.'"

Luckily Gabriel's backside didn't feel it the first time Gabriel called Wayne, "Duke."

"He just shook his head," Gabriel said, with a laugh.

Gabriel played the part of "Blue Boy" and then some. When it came time for the rough-and-tumble stuff, Gabriel didn't defer to others.

"I did my own stunts because you could make more money, double of what they were going to pay you," Gabriel said. "So I hung out with the stunt guys and those guys were as tough as anyone you would meet."

Wayne had his indispensable swagger and presence, Gabriel added.

"He was the man," Gabriel said. "Whatever needed to be done, he would get it done.

Which means Wayne's little feet were in constant motion.

"He was 6-foot-3 and 250 pounds but the first thing I noticed about him was his size 8 shoe," Gabriel said.

Gabriel's other acting credits included appearing in *Ironside*, *The Misadventures of Sheriff Lobo*, and *Gilligan's Island*, where he played a headhunter. Gabriel, with his rugged good looks, was as comfortable with the acting crowd as they were with him.

Once Gabriel was invited to play in a celebrity golf tournament in Palm Springs. In the foursome ahead of him was an entertainer and three June Taylor dancers.

"It just so happens we're playing behind Jackie Gleason," Gabriel said. "I'm playing with [comedian] George Gobel and it takes a while because at every hole he would tell a joke."

Seriously, though, few played through like Gleason.

"Jackie had a Rolls-Royce golf cart and it was pulling a little bar," Gabriel said. "One time he hit a shot up on the rocks and the June Taylor dancers took out a red carpet so he could walk up to his ball. What an experience that was."

Chapter 3

BILLY TRUAX

Rams at Vikings—December 27, 1969

BIRTH DATE:	July 15, 1943
HOMETOWN:	Gulfport, Mississippi
RESIDENCE:	Kearney, Nebraska
JERSEY NO.:	87
POSITION:	Tight end
HEIGHT:	6 foot 5
WEIGHT:	240 pounds

The Run-Up

Billy Truax would have the game of his life on a frigid field in Bloomington, Minnesota. How a country boy from Biloxi, Mississippi, got there is quite a tale.

A star at Louisiana State University, Truax was drafted by the Cleveland Browns in 1964.

"There were twelve [NFL] teams and twenty rounds of the draft," Truax said. "The Browns selected Paul Warfield with their No. 1 pick and me with their No. 2 pick. Of that draft, eleven guys made it to the Hall of Fame, which is the most ever from one draft. It was a really good draft."

Though Truax had been a successful tight end at LSU, the Browns had other plans for him.

"That was Jim Brown's [next to last] year," Truax recalled. "They put me at linebacker, which they admitted later that they had me out of position. They were trying to make something out of me that I couldn't be."

The depth chart showed Truax was far down the list for outside linebackers. Then after one snap, he wasn't on the chart at all.

"One of the backs ran a swing route from the backfield and I went after him," Truax said, "But I tore up my left hamstring from top to bottom; it just ripped. I was in rehabilitation for about six weeks, which was just about to the end of training camp."

With his health intact, Truax got an invitation to join the College All-Stars against the Bears in Chicago. He recalled playing for the legendary Otto Graham in that game.

Unfortunately for Truax, upon his return to Cleveland, he learned that his career as a Brown was crumbling like a cookie.

"When I got back to Cleveland, [Browns owner] Art Modell called me down to Cleveland Municipal Stadium on a Sunday afternoon," Truax said. "I had just gotten settled in, was newly married, and had moved into a rental house.

"I didn't know what was up and I walked into his big office and he was there with one of the personnel guys."

Truax, his Southern manners never far away, greeted Modell in a cordial manner.

"How you doing?" Truax asked. "What's up?"

Modell shuffled through his stack of papers, looked up, and said: "We just traded you to the Los Angeles Rams."

Truax was stunned.

"You talk about your heart leaping into your throat," he said. "I went home and told my wife and the next day or so we went to L.A."

It was immediate culture shock, and not just because of the abundance of sunshine. Told to report to the team's practice field in the San Fernando Valley, Truax did a double-take upon arrival.

"It was just a regular city park," he said. "There wasn't even a designated football field there. They just put up 2x4s and put hooks on them and that was your locker. We used a garden hose to shower with after practices."

Harland Svare was the coach, with Truax among nearly a dozen rookies seeking to catch his eye. Truax stuck around, but he got stuck behind Marlin McKeever.

"I didn't play," Truax said. "Harland was in love with McKeever, a big USC guy, so I was on special teams and that was about it."

Not much came Truax's way the next year either.

Every team needs a tight end with reliable hands and Truax fit the bill. Truax had a big game in the 1969 playoffs against the Vikings, although Minnesota would prevail in one of the most heartbreaking games in Rams history.

"I was on a two-year, no-cut contract so I was there for two years whether they liked it or not," he said.

Owner Dan Reeves had grown tired of Svare after the Rams went 4–10 in 1965.

Truax had become weary with the game, too. His two-year deal up, he headed for home in Baton Rouge, Louisiana.

"I decided I had had enough," he said. "But the Rams hired George Allen to coach and he called me up and said there was going to be new life with the team. Still, I told him I thought I had had enough and I didn't want to do this anymore."

Allen kept working on Truax.

"I know you had a bad experience, but we were hoping you could hang on," Allen said. "We think you can play in the league and I will talk to some people about giving you a raise. We would like to have you back."

The additional greenbacks got Truax's attention. With a $3,000 increase, Truax headed west once again.

"I went back, but Marlin is still starting," Truax said. "But he has an accident during training camp and he was out for about six weeks. I got to play and started every game after that."

Allen was true to his word.

"He was a players' coach," Truax said. "But it came down to if you produced, you played. If you didn't, he had no use for you. That is when you learn it is a pretty much a cutthroat business."

The Game

By Billy Truax

I was lucky to be there at the time where we had George Allen as a coach and a lot of great football players on the team. But I think if I have to remember one game, it was the divisional playoff game against the Minnesota Vikings in 1969 in Bloomington.

We had been there all week as George Allen took us down there a week ahead of time; we spent Christmas near the stadium. The Vikings had gone down to Florida to get ready—they already knew about the cold weather.

But we were West Coast guys and Allen thought we needed to get over there and practice in it and get used to it.

On game day, it was 10 degrees with high winds. It was a rough weather day, but they had to play in it, too. I had a pretty good game, as I caught five passes and scored a touchdown.

We got off to a great start and we were feeling pretty good about things. I caught a 2-yard touchdown pass and we went in at halftime ahead 17–7. But then I don't know what happened, as we came out kind of flat for the second half. We couldn't get much going.

Allen kind of wore us out that year. He believed in long practices. Review, review, review. He was always making sure everything was in order. He hadn't learned the lesson of easing up a bit later in the season. Instead it was keeping the foot on the pedal. There was never any concern about fatigue and that you needed rest to recover and stay as fresh as you can.

So I don't know if it was due to the fact of being on [the] road the whole week. But we were all excited and fired up, winning that game and we were definitely ready to go. We came out and played well and dominated them.

But after halftime, we kind of cooled off and it was kind of hard to get it going again. It was their home field and those guys they just got off fast. As the game unfolded, we just couldn't get much momentum.

You have to remember we had a heck of a team. Roman Gabriel was the MVP that year and we had seven guys make the Pro Bowl [Bob Brown, Deacon Jones, Merlin Olsen, Roman Gabriel, Tom Mack, Maxie Baughan, and Charlie Cowan].

And four guys on defense were All-Pro. Deacon and Merlin were the noteworthy guys, but we also had Ed Meador and Maxie.

Late in that game I had a chance to catch one last pass. I was partially open coming across the middle, but Karl Kassulke had one arm on my left arm so I just had the other arm to make the catch. If I would have made the catch, it would have given us a first down. Instead of it being fourth down, we would have had the ball and a first down and maybe been in position to kick a field goal and take it into overtime.

If I would have made just one more move . . . I think about that play almost every night.

It was a middle route that we had run before, where we made it look like a standard running play. It stretched the formation on both sides; we had two tight ends in, with Bob Klein being on the opposite side.

For my 2-yard touchdown pass we ran that route down near the goal line. We faked to the running back and we would delay coming out for our route. [Truax also had receptions of 18 and 16 yards on the scoring drive.]

For the touchdown, it was kind of a falling-down catch because I didn't want to take any chances of dropping the ball with the ice and snow. It was a good throw and I fell right into it. It was a good catch.

Also in the game, toward the end of it, Roman was going to throw me a . . . route where I would come off the ball looking. But Alan Page, instead of rushing the passer, he backed off and intercepted the ball right at midfield. That was basically our last possession. He ran it to the sidelines and when he got up he said some smart-ass remark to Roman.

I remember Joe Kapp jumping over Richie Petitbon, hurdling him and going in for a fourth-quarter touchdown. Hurdling was supposed to be illegal, but they didn't call it.

On another call a Viking caught a pass and then got up to run because no one had touched him. Jack Pardee ran him down and hit him hard from behind, but they called 15 yards for unnecessary roughness for some reason.

We were slipping and sliding and we got some bad calls. There was a mix-up on downs once.

It was exciting and devastating as well. We were all sick and tired after the game because it was such a brutal, brutal loss. But they came back and beat us.

The thing was that it was such a great team and all our guys were at their peak. After 1969, we never got any closer than that. The next year we went 9–4–1 and didn't make the playoffs.

The Aftermath

Legendary CBS broadcaster Jack Whitaker was poking around for Billy Truax at the Vikings' Metropolitan Stadium after another divisional playoff game there on Christmas Day in 1971.

"He came into the locker room and to my locker to look me up," Truax said. "He wanted me to talk about me coming back there and being able to win."

Truax was exorcising an old Rams demon in prevailing at the Met, the site of the gut-wrenching loss in the 1969 playoffs.

Although on this frigid December day Truax was sticking pins in his Vikings voodoo doll as a Cowboy. After the 1970 season, a new sheriff rode into Los Angeles with coach Tom Prothro. Truax was among the posse that rode out.

"The Rams fired Allen and that was a surprise, and they hired Tommy Prothro from UCLA," Truax said. "He comes in there and wants to clean house and put in his system with all his people, but I didn't think much of it. I had no idea I would ever be traded to the Dallas Cowboys."

Allen was headed to the Washington Redskins and the future was now for Truax. Could he tag along, he asked Allen?

"I asked him to take me, but he said they already had another team lined up for a trade," Truax said.

Truax went to Dallas, where the Southern California vibe was tougher to find than passes pointed toward tight ends.

"I had been in L.A. for seven years and Dallas was a whole new locker room, a different spot with a different soul.

"Everyone talked about how complicated coach [Tom] Landry's offense was going to be. But Landry was all about the 'Doomsday Defense' and I didn't have to worry about that.

"There wasn't a whole lot to do as a tight end. You either blocked for a run or ran a route inside. I don't know what is so complicated about that."

Maybe there was a reason the tight end was marginalized.

"Bob Hayes and Calvin Hill were their go-to guys," Truax said. "They were pretty good."

Truax's sidekick was Mike Ditka. For the most part they were human shuttles, alternating in relaying plays from Landry to quarterback Roger Staubach.

That included Super Bowl VI, when the Cowboys faced the Miami Dolphins. Although in that 24–3 win the tight end tandem once took matters into their own hands.

"It was my turn to go in and Tom called for a tight end reverse," Truax said. "But my left knee was really, really bad so Tom called me back off the field to change the play.

"But I knew the play would work, so I told Mike and he turned around and stayed on the field. He ran it around the left side for 17 yards and almost scored."

Winning a Super Bowl in New Orleans' Tulane Stadium was high cotton for a former LSU star and Mississippi native. But it's not clear if it eclipsed that win two rounds earlier in Minnesota, where Truax had an old score to settle.

"Being able to win that game was kind of a crystallizing moment of not winning it when I was with the Rams," Truax said. "It was the next step. Like yeah, vindication, to finally win in Minnesota."

Chapter 4

RICHIE PETITBON

Rams at Vikings—December 27, 1969

BIRTH DATE:	April 18, 1938
HOMETOWN:	New Orleans, Louisiana
RESIDENCE:	Vienna, Virginia
JERSEY NO.:	17
POSITION:	Strong safety
HEIGHT:	6 foot 3
WEIGHT:	206 pounds

The Run-Up

Richie Petitbon was a New Orleans feel-good story, the local football star who stayed near home to play at Loyola of the South and Tulane.

If you're from the South, it's not surprising to have a native sticking close by.

So it wasn't a stretch when Petitbon tried to get back to his Southern roots despite being a star for the Chicago Bears from 1959 to 1968. Petitbon was a four-time Pro Bowler, and his 38 interceptions are the second-most in franchise history. One of his highlights with the Bears came against the Rams, when he set a club record with a 101-yard interception return.

Chicago was grand, but it just wasn't the South.

"That was a great sports town," Petitbon said. "But I wanted to go to New Orleans and play for the Saints."

Despite the sad-sack Saints having quarterback Archie Manning and little else, Petitbon longed for a return to the Crescent City. He tried to play out his contract with the Bears. Instead he was acquired by a coach who was at every intersection of Petitbon's NFL career: George Allen.

"He was the defensive coordinator when I was with Chicago," Petitbon said. "Then he got me to Los Angeles. Then he would get me to Washington."

Petitbon, a hard-hitting safety, didn't get his wish to land with New Orleans. Those dreams of playing for the Saints were replaced by the reality of become a Ram. Petitbon was headed to the West Coast to a new team. But he would be greeted by a familiar face in Allen.

"I guess he liked me because we always won," Petitbon said, while laughing. "And he could recognize talent."

Upon his arrival in Los Angeles, Petitbon cemented his relationship with Allen. That circumstance led Petitbon to a coaching career that spanned nearly two decades.

Petitbon never let the good times roll in New Orleans. But he had some in L.A., too, including the game of his life, a postseason matchup against the Vikings.

The Game

By Richie Petitbon

We both had good teams, and this game was for the Western Conference Championship.

Our defense was really good. We had Deacon Jones, Merlin Olsen, Coy Bacon, Diron Talbert, guys like that. We had a defense, yes, and it was a good defense.

That was a good Rams team, it really was. I do remember, though, that we got beat in Minnesota.

The Vikings had Joe Kapp and he was a great quarterback, a great winner. I'm not sure of his talent level or anything like that, but he got the job done, and you have to give him credit for that, no question.

Our secondary, though, was a good one. Eddie Meador was the free safety and I played strong safety. We had Clancy Williams and Jim Nettles as the cornerbacks.

And then with our pass rush, led by Deacon and Merlin, that made things easier. That helped cover up a multitude of sins.

We mixed things up against Kapp in our coverages. That was always one of our staples.

If you could relate it to a pitcher in baseball, well, we had more than one pitch. That was important. Because no matter how good you are, you have to be changing it up a little bit.

31

That was a long time ago, but I know we didn't give them just one coverage—not against Kapp.

We always played good games against the Vikings and this one was a good one, too. I recovered a fumble from Bill Brown somewhere around midfield early in the game.

Gabriel, he was such a good quarterback, but he got intercepted by Carl Eller and he returned it for a touchdown. But they brought it back because Alan Page was called for being offsides.

I think we traded touchdowns and then Bruce Gossett had a field goal. We are winning 10–7.

Right before halftime Gabriel started completing passes to Billy Truax. He hit Truax before halftime for a score and we were up 17–7 going into the locker room.

Kapp got going a little bit—he was a winner—in the second half and they scored to make it 17–14. But our defense makes some stops and Eddie Meador intercepted a pass; Eddie was a really good player. But we don't score off the turnover.

On the next defensive series I get an interception and we get the ball down inside the Vikings' 40-yard line. We got the ball down close, but we had to settle for a field goal.

So that's two turnovers and we only get three points.

Instead of it being maybe 31–14 if we would have scored two touchdowns off the two interceptions, or at least 24–14 if we scored off my interception, it was a lot closer. We don't get any touchdowns, just that field goal, and the score is 20–14 going into the fourth quarter.

We didn't do much in the last quarter. The Vikings went ahead, there was a safety, and then our last chance ended in a tipped ball, which was intercepted.

I'm not sure who got it—that was a long time ago. But I remember being disappointed because that 1969 Rams team was the best team I played on.

The Aftermath

Richie Petitbon had established himself in Chicago, but he embraced playing for the Rams. Yet it was a loveaffair that would last a mere two years, as he was traded to the Washington Redskins after the 1970 season.

"I really enjoyed my time in Los Angeles," he said. "It was fun."

Even if the game of his life with the Rams came with a broken heart.

That 1969 Western Conference Championship loss to the Minnesota Vikings eliminated the team that, to this day, Petitbon says is the best he played on.

Despite the defeat, that set the foundation for a bond between Petitbon and his fellow Rams. Sometimes in the toughest of losses a connection is formed, one that can be among the hardest to break. All these years later, Petitbon rattled off many of his teammates' names, admiration accompanying every syllable.

So when Petitbon returned to the Los Angeles Memorial Coliseum with Washington in 1971 to face the Rams, it meant the world to him.

"Among the most important games in my career was actually against the Rams," Petitbon said. "It was when I was with the Redskins and we came back to play the Rams on a Monday night game. I remember that one."

Revenge? Petitbon is too much of a Southern gentleman to let that unseemly thought cross his cerebral mind.

Then again . . .

"I was stung by being traded from the Rams," Petitbon admitted. "So when we came back and then we beat them the next year, that was one of the most rewarding games I had ever played in. It was about my pride, so sure, there was a little bit of extra motivation."

Petitbon was always hyped to play at the Coliseum, whether he was trying to settle a score or prevent one. There was something about "The Grand Old Lady," which was what some locals called the Rams' historic home.

"I always had good games at the Coliseum," Petitbon said. "I don't know why, but even when I was with the Bears and we would come out to play the Rams, I would play well. It was a good experience. I always felt right at home there."

Washington got right cozy on that surreal Monday night in an NFL homecoming like few others.

Redskins coach George Allen, who was fired from the Rams after the 1970 season, along with numerous other former Rams, returned to the old haunts in an impressive fashion. They defeated L.A., 38–24, which knocked the Rams out of the playoffs.

A casual Rams fan might have been confused regarding for which team to cheer that December night.

Defensive stalwarts Jack Pardee, Myron Pottios, Diron Talbert, and of course, Petitbon, were among the ex-Rams on Allen's squad running out through the Coliseum's well-worn tunnel.

"That was a good win," said Petitbon, still sounding satisfied several decades later.

Petitbon was on the right side because, once again, he was on Allen's side. For the third time, on his third and final team in Petitbon's 14-year career, Allen was his coach.

After making his mark with the Chicago Bears, Petitbon (17) was a monster in the Rams' secondary. A cerebral player who would become an NFL head coach, Petitbon was a key part of the 1969 team which went 11-3 and considered by many as among the best Rams squads in franchise history. Petitbon tied for a team-high five interceptions that year. (AP Photo/Larry Stoddard)

When Petitbon was drafted out of Tulane by Chicago in 1959, Allen was on the Bears' defensive coaching staff.

When Petitbon was acquired by Los Angeles in 1969, it was Allen as the coach pulling the strings to guarantee the reunion.

When Allen was unceremoniously shown the door after the 1970 season, Petitbon became part of the legendary "Over the Hill Gang" that Allen constructed in a flurry of wheeling-and-dealing in returning Washington to relevance.

"I kind of followed him around," Petitbon said with a chuckle.

Although Petitbon didn't anticipate tagging along on the L.A.-to-D.C. route. When Rams owner Dan Reeves decided to fire Allen in favor of Tommy Prothro, Petitbon thought his days with Allen were finished.

"I know I was at the end of my career, but I still had a little mileage left," said Petitbon, a year removed from intercepting five passes and recovering a fumble. "So being traded was a surprise."

What didn't cause double-takes, especially from Petitbon, was Allen being an immediate success in resurrecting Washington's fortunes. In Allen's debut year in D.C. he produced Washington's first winning record in 15 seasons. In his second year, and Petitbon's last as a player, Allen not only directed the club to its initial playoff appearance in 26 years but also to Super Bowl VII.

"I'm still not sure why the Rams ever got rid of George," Petitbon said, a question that has long puzzled Rams followers. "I guess some things you just can't explain."

Petitbon, whose coaching resume would include being Washington's head coach, admired the quirky, but innovative, Allen.

"George was really ahead of the game," Petitbon said. "Some of the things that he did wasn't being done until he started doing it.

"The nickel defense? It's hard to believe, but nobody used to put a fifth defense back in games in passing situations until George did it.

"Those pass-rushers? Guys that played on the defensive line used to never come out back then. But in passing situations, George would put in the pass-rush specialists. It always seemed like George was one step ahead of everybody."

In 1972, Petitbon's body was wearing down with his career winding down. His last game was Super Bowl VII, when the Dolphins kept their pristine season intact at the expense of Washington with a 14–7 victory.

But Petitbon recalled a perfect pass that didn't find its target. Much like Roman Gabriel's attempt, which was deflected and picked off by Alan Page in the closing minute of the Rams' 1974 playoff loss to the Minnesota Vikings.

That changed the complexion of Petitbon's most memorable Rams game.

In Super Bowl VII, a batted down pass did likewise. If it's completed, maybe the Dolphins' clean record would have shown a blemish.

"What I remember about that is Jerry Smith was wide open in the end zone and back then the goal post was not at back of the end zone but on the goal line," Petitbon said. "Billy Kilmer threw a great pass and he was going to complete it to Smith, but it hit the goal post.

"It was a great pass, but Kilmer couldn't have done that if he tried. That actually happened in a Super Bowl. If Smith would have caught that pass, things might have turned out different."

The ball bounced Petitbon's way after he left the Rams despite his disappointment in being peddled to the opposite coast.

Petitbon became a celebrated defensive coordinator in Washington lore, with his units helping bring three Super Bowl titles to the nation's capital.

By George, Washington was the place for Petitbon. And in some ways, it was because of Allen, a former Rams coach whose affinity for Petitbon had a significant impact.

"Let me say this about George Allen," Petitbon said. "I think his teams always played up to the best of their ability. He had a knack for getting the best out of people and that is what coaching is all about."

Chapter 5

FRED DRYER

Rams at Bears—September 24, 1972

BIRTH DATE:	July 6, 1946
HOMETOWN:	Hawthorne, California
RESIDENCE:	Los Angeles, California
JERSEY NO.:	89
POSITION:	Defensive end
HEIGHT:	6 foot 6
WEIGHT:	240 pounds

The Run-Up

That Fred Dryer played for the Rams could have been part of a Hollywood script. The standout player from Lawndale High and El Camino College making his way to the local pro team seemed to be in the stars.

But maybe Dryer doesn't land with the Rams, via a trade with the New York Giants, unless he stiff-arms Florida State after his sophomore season at El Camino.

"I was on my way to Florida State and then something happened," Dryer said. "They called that summer and said I needed to get down there and enroll in junior college and take like a handball class or something. They said if I didn't do that, I was not going to Florida State.

"So at the very last minute I call down to San Diego State. I talk with [defensive coach] John Madden and it ends up that he picks me up and puts me in school."

San Diego State was Division 1-AA but it was a first-class program. With coach Don Coryell directing a passing attack seldom seen at any level, the Aztecs were dominant.

And Dryer said the popular Coryell's influence on him was never matched by another coach.

"The older I got the more I realized that," Dryer said. "He just loved his players and the players loved him. I know it's a cliché that everyone says that about their coaches but we really did because he did in a different way. He was just so optimistic that he had a way of freeing you up so you could enjoy the game."

In Coryell's San Diego State stint from 1961 to 1972, the Aztecs were 104-19-2. They had three undefeated seasons, including Dryer's senior year in 1968.

"That was when I had the most fun game of my life," Dryer said. "And it was against Southern Mississippi."

Coryell's innovative brand of football was thrilling to watch. But few people knew about it.

"A lot of schools, certainly outside of Southern California, weren't really aware of what San Diego State was doing at the time and understood what was going on down there," Dryer said.

"You had a very offensive-minded prolific genius coach in Coryell who had an all-star lineup of coaches: Joe Gibbs, John Madden, Ernie Zampese, Rod Dowhower, and the like.

"And we ran an offense that was spread with five wide receivers in the passing attack."

The Aztecs got after teams mostly with junior-college transfers. It was a hungry group of players that the bigger schools (i.e. USC and UCLA) didn't think were good enough.

"Coryell was putting together all the players that were kind of rejected by the Pac-8 schools," Dryer said. "All of this leads up to the Southern Mississippi game."

The Golden Eagles had lost three straight to Ole Miss, Memphis, and Louisiana Tech and were seeking a cupcake in the Division 1-AA Aztecs, a 40-point underdog. Southern Miss coach Pie Vann apologized in advance for likely having to run the score up on San Diego State to quiet the restless hometown boosters in Hattiesburg. Vann's remarks came at the coaches' press conference the Friday before the game.

Coryell was seated at the dais, biting his tongue.

"We'll show up and we'll play tough," Coryell said curtly, and quickly sat down.

The Aztecs had already done their film study on the Golden Eagles. Dryer knew Vann's premonition wouldn't fly.

"They were playing in a three-deep zone with a safety in the middle and they were going to do that against five wideouts," Dryer said. "This was not to be believed. It was a classic mismatch of the different styles. But Las Vegas [oddsmakers] didn't really know about it and the schools down South certainly didn't."

A ticked Coryell greeted his players at that Friday's practice.

"He was [expletive] crazy," Dryer said. "He was spitting all over the place and calling them sons of a [guns]. It was wild."

The savvy Dryer realized there was more than a signature win to be gained. Back at his frat house, they talked a member into driving to Las Vegas and taking those 40 points and picking San Diego State.

"We're going to make a bunch of money," Dryer said. "We told him to get his [tail] over there and make the bet."

Saturday arrived and Southern Miss couldn't believe its eyes— during warmups. The Aztecs were wearing all black uniforms and doing back flips off the bench.

"They were all laughing at us," Dryer said.

Soon the joke was on them.

"Sure enough I intercepted a quick toss on a pitchout and I just take off for like 30 yards for the first score and that started it. [Wide receiver] Tommy Nettles [caught] four touchdowns, Dennis Shaw threw for seven touchdowns and 500 yards and we had like 600 yards in offense. We beat them 68–7, so figuring the 40 points we were giving, I always called it, 'The 100-point upset.'"

But Dryer became queasy in the third quarter when peeking into the San Diego Stadium stands, which were rocking with excitement.

"They were literally going crazy it was such a beat-down," Dryer said. "And I was in the huddle thinking, 'Man, we're going to make a [expletive] lot of money.'"

Dryer was a force on the field and a character off it. Not many Rams enjoyed their time more in Los Angeles than Dryer, with his flair for dramatic plays and outlandish statements.

Want to bet?

"Just then I looked up in the stands and saw the guy we entrusted to go to Vegas and make the bet," Dryer said. "He was in the stands and not in Vegas because he got drunk Friday night and never made it over there."

That proves someone has to get to Vegas for their actions to stay there.

No bet. No money. No problem.

"We pounded the [crap] out of Southern Miss," Dryer said. "It was by far the most fun I had in a game in my life.

"And who knows what might have happened if I had gone down to Florida State? I might have ended up on a tuna boat to Cuba.

"Instead I got to stay home, play in San Diego, and be on the ground floor of a great program under an iconic coach."

The Game

By Fred Dryer

When you look back on the game of your life, well, if I'm talking about personally it's probably the two safeties I had against the Green Bay Packers in the Coliseum in 1973. But that is kind of self-serving.

I think of a game that is maybe wrapped around the instances. And one particular game was in my first year with the Rams in 1972.

Tommy Prothro was the coach and he was as eccentric as you could imagine. He was very smart—a championship bridge player, and he liked his cards.

But he would do peculiar things. We went to practice on a Wednesday before our game one week against San Francisco. He walked into the meeting room and said. "We should all take off and go to the beach."

He said it while sitting there smoking. He was always smoking and often when he was talking there would be long pauses.

Then he said, "Well, why you don't you go to the beach?"

Of course no one moved—we were just staring at him.

"Go on, get out of here."

So we sprinted out of the place.

We couldn't believe it, and just then [owner] Carroll Rosenbloom and [general manager] Don Klosterman drive up to Blair Field for practice. They had driven over from our Los Angeles office on Pico Boulevard.

Carroll said, "What the hell is going on?"

No one had told them because it was just a spur of the moment thing from Prothro. They wouldn't have made that drive if they had known he was going to do that.

But that was telling of the crazy year, the mass hilarity that took place with Prothro.

We beat San Francisco that week, but the oddity was we would finish 6–7–1 and Prothro got fired.

But the game in 1972 that stands out is when we were in Chicago at Soldier Field. We were in these [crappy] locker rooms. They are literally high school lockers we were dressing at and we can't even put anything in there. They had to lay out our uniforms on the floor. They are not hanging out in the locker like they normally do.

During pregame [Roman Gabriel] was having a tough time loosening up. He was using this flex-like tubing exercise but nothing was working. He was a workout fanatic—he worked out all the time.

But on this day his arm was taking longer to get loosened up. I just remember being in the locker room with him and it was really cramped, with a bunch of reporters and it was filled with smoke because Prothro was always smoking.

It wasn't like these modern-day locker rooms—it was really cramped.

Gabe walks back into the room and sees one of the team doctors. He asks for a shot to get his arm loosened up. He said he was having soreness when throwing the ball.

So the doctor gets the needle out and he sticks Gabe on the inside of his elbow. But he misses the designated target and kills Gabe's arm. His arm is just hanging down by his side.

I mean Gabe now can't even pick up a football and he yells at the doctor, "What the [heck] are you doing?"

The doctor grabs his arm and said, "Oh, you can't feel that?"

Gabe yells, "I can't feel a [expletive] thing!"

Trainer Cash Birdwell runs off and gets Prothro. He shuffles through the crowd of people to the very back of the room and he tells everyone to get the hell out.

Prothro asked the doctor what happened and the doctor said: "I just [expletive] your quarterback's arm up."

I'm standing in the hallway and I get wind of this. I go find Pete Beathard, our backup quarterback, and tell him, "Hey Pete, you better get loose." He looks at me like I'm crazy and just then Prothro walks in and said, "You're playing right now."

The offense got the [crap] pounded out of them. Beathard completed 6 of 12 passes for 46 yards and an interception in a 13–13 tie.

I remember sitting on the bench during the game and the doctor asks Gabe how his arm felt now.

Gabe said, "[Bleep] you. My arm is killing me."

[Gabriel made a brief appearance. He completed 1 of 5 passes for 19 yards, with an interception.]

It was just a crazy, crazy year with a crazy coach and that is the game I remember.

The real fun started in 1973, when Chuck Knox took over. But it was that 1972 season, and that game in Soldier Field, that I remember most.

The Aftermath

Fred Dryer almost ended up on the working side of the bar where everyone knows your name. His playing career was winding down in 1981 and with his proximity to Hollywood, Dryer thought about acting.

"I started testing for the networks and my real big break came when the Charles brothers, Glen and Les, and Jim Burrows were writing *Cheers*," he said. "They asked me if we tested you for the lead and if you got it would you quit football? I said, 'Sure, I'll make that commitment,' and they tested me [and] I did real well."

Unlike Pete Beathard back at Soldier Field, Dryer was ready for his close-up.

Dryer was among three finalists, along with Ted Danson and Will Devane, for the part as barkeep Sam Malone.

"It was really between Ted and I and they went with Ted because he had more experience," Dryer said. "That was a good choice, but I could have played the hell out of it."

Dryer went on to appear in four episodes as Dave Richards, Danson's former Red Sox teammate who had become an obnoxious sports anchor.

But Dryer's real mark was courtesy of another show. The man known for lowering his pads into quarterbacks for the Rams delivered the lowdown to the bad guys as a member of the Los Angeles Police Department.

Dryer became Sgt. Rick Hunter in the crime-stopping series *Hunter*, a TV staple from 1984 to 1991. But in the production's early stages, Dryer was derailed by a familiar foe.

It was *Dallas*, only minus the Cowboys.

Maybe these losses didn't equal that of the 1980 Rams, the defending NFC champions, being eliminated in the playoffs by Dallas. But Dryer was the only one who experienced both.

On TV, *Hunter* was slotted against the popular *Dallas* and the ratings reflected the new show's struggles.

"We were opposite *Dallas* on Friday nights for ten episodes," Dryer said. "Then [NBC executive] Brandon Tartikoff moved it to Saturday nights and we took off. It just exploded and we were up in the top ten for a while.

"What the show had was a dynamic between Stepfanie Kramer and myself. We got along so well, it was a lot of fun, and people enjoyed watching us. It doesn't matter what the show is about, having that chemistry is 90 percent of it."

So Dryer became Hunter, and the Southern California native really did live part of a Hollywood script. But just like winning on the field, conquering Hollywood wasn't as easy as it appeared.

"You have to be lucky enough to stay committed to it and stay in it long enough that you can survive the down side," Dryer said. "There's a lot of down side to it.

"I had no idea what I was getting into. I thought you just got your [Screen Actors Guild] card and drive to Hollywood and do the best you can. But you get kicked around some."

Dryer approached it with the seriousness of playing in the NFL. There were no shortcuts, as he took acting lessons and tested his fortitude by sticking with it.

"My whole interest was really to learn a skill, a craft, and to understand what acting was and what it wasn't," he said. "I had to see whether or not I could make a living at it. If I didn't fit in or make it, I wasn't going to flounder about doing it.

"Then I got *Hunter* and figured I could make some kind of a run out of this."

To that, we say, "Cheers."

Chapter 6

TOM MACK

Rams at Vikings—December 29, 1974

BIRTH DATE:	November 1, 1943
HOMETOWN:	Cleveland, Ohio
RESIDENCE:	Henderson, Nevada
JERSEY NO.:	65
POSITION:	Right guard
HEIGHT:	6 foot 3
WEIGHT:	250 pounds

The Run-Up

Tom Mack had his sights set on being a star split end at Michigan.

And he might have been, except for one small obstacle.

"I couldn't catch," Mack said. "So I wasn't going to play."

Offensive line coach Tony Mason saw just that after Mack's lackluster sophomore season. Mason sidled up to Mack one day with a question.

"Do you want to play offensive tackle?" Mason said.

"If I get to play," Mack replied, "I would love to."

So Mack switched positions and flipped a college career that was going nowhere fast.

While overlooking Mack's stone hands, Mason spotted a rock of a lineman.

"He saw that I was extremely quick and fast," Mack said.

What Mack wasn't was a quick study, with his unreliable mitts now in the dirt.

"I guess I was either dumb or tenacious," Mack said. "I spent a lot of time learning, trying, and eventually I got the hang of it.

"I don't know how I did it, but I was voted the most improved player award in the spring. So it ended up being a nice story. I'm glad I did it."

Mack would start seven games for the 1964 team at right tackle, as the Wolverines tried to erase the memories of their previous two seasons. They had won just five games over that span, but with numerous starters returning, there was hope in Ann Arbor that better days were ahead.

"But there are a million things to be proven before anyone can point to us as a team that can go all the way," coach Bump Elliott said before the 1964 season, in trying to dampen the enthusiasm.

He wasn't talking about Mack, but he could have been.

The Wolverines, though, were the real deal. With Mack contributing to a veteran offensive line, Michigan won its first Big 10 Conference title since 1950. The Wolverines' only loss was to the Bob Griese-led Purdue team as Michigan steamrolled toward the Rose Bowl.

There to greet them wasn't a little old lady from Pasadena, but a little overmatched Oregon State team from Corvallis. Michigan was an 11-point favorite and did more than cover in thumping the Beavers 34–7.

"There were times when our players blasted Michigan players at full speed and only wound up flat on their backs with the other people on top of them," Oregon State coach Tommy Prothro said. "I've never seen such hitting."

Prothro *could* have been talking about Mack, who was just getting started.

The next season Michigan took a step back while Mack went upward and onward. While the Wolverines' encore to their Rose Bowl victory only produced a 4-6 mark, Mack was named to the All Big-10 team.

The one-time fresh face on the line had gradually become a hot commodity in the eyes of the NFL. The Los Angeles Rams made him their first-round pick and No. 2 overall. It was the last time that the NFL and the AFL drafted separately.

"It was a big surprise when I ended up getting drafted so high," said Mack, who was also picked by the AFL's Miami Dolphins. Mack decided on the more established NFL, despite the fact that the Dolphins, an expansion franchise, had made a supreme effort to lure him to South Beach.

Mack played in 184 consecutive games, as the rock in which the Rams' offensive line was built around as he would go on to the Pro Football Hall of Fame. The 11-time Pro Bowler Mack's leadership qualities matched his ability to keep Rams' ball carriers from harm's way.

Mack blossomed only because he embraced Coach Mason's suggestions to move in closer to the center. Of course Mack put in the work, which paid off for someone who mostly collected splinters his sophomore season.

Before the game of his life, Mack received the advice that changed his course.

"That was the big break of my life," Mack said.

The Game

By Tom Mack

We were playing for the NFC Championship in 1974. We were at Minnesota and this was a crazy game.

James Harris probably had one of the greatest plays ever in the game. He scrambled around, and he wasn't a scrambling quarterback, and he hit Harold Jackson on a long pass in the fourth quarter.

We were trailing, 7–3, but we ended up on the 1-yard line. Actually we had less than a yard to score.

We had controlled the game and I had done well against Alan Page.

But we are on the 1-yard line and we go to a long snap, like you do when you are going to have a quarterback sneak.

Page jumps offsides and knocks me over backward. The official comes in from the side and said, "Someone moved on the inside and it must have been the guard."

I said, "That's bull because I literally didn't move." But it put us back to the 5-yard line.

I told [Rams] coach Chuck Knox that I would bet him a game check that I hadn't moved. Afterward he came up to me and said,

"You're right, but I'm not giving you a game check" (which was $4,000).

Page never talked about it but he knew what happened. As it turned out if you look at the game film the tight end on our side moved, but he was allowed to move. He's the only guy [allowed to do that]. If he puts his hand down on the ground he can pick it back up and go in motion or shift.

All he did was shift because it was a long-count snap. Page blew past the line and went offsides.

I sure as hell didn't move. I was getting ready to fire underneath Page; he knew it right away.

It almost felt like the game was fixed because that call was the game. There were three or four penalties against us by this one guy. Usually the calls are made and spread out by the whole officiating crew, but this guy made like three or four calls that he usually wouldn't make.

I think he was one of the line judges; it wasn't the umpire that will call you for holding and movement inside because he is the guy right behind the linebacker.

That guy didn't have anything to say about it.

So I'm sitting there and I really felt I had a great game, but we lost, 14–10. Then I'm sitting there sucking hide feeling like I lost the game. I had to say, "Blame this one on me because it was my mistake."

But at the same time Knox made a point of saying, "Mack never moved." But so what. The game is over, they are in the playoffs.

But it was a smart play on Page's part. What did he have to lose? A half-inch?

You can feel a guy move if he moves and I didn't feel [offensive tackle] Charlie [Cowan] move and he didn't feel me move.

The thing with Page was he was going to try to run you over so you try to get him off balance. I was 250 pounds at the time, which was big enough. Because being agile was more important than having brute strength.

I've got a great picture of me blocking Alan where I literally would punch him with both arms in the chest and he is almost falling over backward. When he did that, it gave you time and it made him restart again.

But on that play where I didn't move we were moved back to the 5-yard line. Then on the next play James Harris gets his pass tipped and it is intercepted so we ended up losing.

When you lose the last game it just eats you alive for the entire offseason. Because it is the last game and you lose, that is all you can think about, the result.

The Aftermath

Tom Mack had switched from a no-good end to a fantastic lineman at Michigan. But the transformation from playing football to fiddling with a nuclear plant?

Please.

In his next line of work, it was imperative he didn't flinch, like he allegedly did that day in Minnesota, though Mack swears he didn't make a mistake in the Rams' 1974 NFC title game loss.

The ex-Ram became an engineer with Bechtel and helped open the Palo Verde Nuclear Generating Station just outside Phoenix.

"I was the project manager on part of it," he said proudly. "It ended up being a great facility and the largest nuclear station in the country."

It was far from smooth sailing at the outset, though.

"I got there in the fall of 1983 and the whole industry was kind of in a moratorium because it was right after the Three Mile Island accident had happened. So basically we had to rewrite all the rules and go back to square one; recheck all of the systems in the plant. You can't imagine what you are going to have to do to go through all that."

A light bulb went on in Mack long before he was pulling levels to generate nuclear power. While others don't ponder a life after football, Mack knew the day would come when the cheering would stop.

"What is really strange is when most guys would leave the game they didn't have another career figured out," Mack said. "So they would hang around the team, but you really can't hang around the team because you aren't part of it anymore. They almost seemed lost."

That's why Mack used to spend time in the Michigan library as often as on its football field. He got his engineering degree before joining the Rams and worked nine offseasons with Bechtel. Cutting his teeth in the industry as a player let him sink his chops into a career that lasted 35 years.

"Bechtel was really nice about it," he said. "But they would make me quit every year when I was a player only to rehire me the next year."

Mack, though, didn't trade in on his notoriety of being an 11-time Pro Bowler who would wind up in the Pro Football Hall of Fame.

Instead, his previous life was one few knew of.

"Bechtel wouldn't tell anyone I was a former football player," he said. "They thought it would reflect badly on them if they had an ex-football player who was an engineer."

Chapter 7

ROD PERRY

Cowboys at Rams—September 17, 1978

BIRTH DATE:	September 11, 1953
HOMETOWN:	Fresno, California
RESIDENCE:	Fresno, California
JERSEY NO.:	49
POSITION:	Cornerback
HEIGHT:	5 foot 9
WEIGHT:	178 pounds

The Run-Up

The knee gave way, as it often did, momentarily, nearly crushing Rod Perry's hopes of playing in college.

"In my next-to-last game as a junior at Hoover, I injured my knee," said Perry, who lived down the street from Fresno's Hoover High School. "But I overcame that."

Perry is the eldest of three sons of Willie and Juanita Perry. He had set his sights on going to UCLA, where he envisioned leading the Bruins to a Rose Bowl victory.

But life often comes with thorns. Perry realized that when he had to miss his senior year of football at Hoover as his knee healed. Perry would play in a prep all-star game at the end of the season, but his planned journey to Westwood from the Raisin Capital of the World took a serious detour.

Playing in the game of his life with the Rams seemed like fiction. But Perry's will was stronger than his wobbly knee, something he would prove time and again to be an integral contributor to some of the best Rams teams in franchise history.

But all that seemed so far away as Perry's knee ached.

UCLA? It didn't come calling with Perry on the mend. So he stayed local and attended Fresno City College.

"I had to battle through it," said Perry, who help lead Fresno City to the 1972 state title.

His knee healed up, and Perry was subsequently recruited by the University of Colorado. Ultimately, Perry re-established himself during his senior year as a top-flight cornerback again, but something also repeated itself: another knee injury.

"I was devastated because I didn't know if I was rated by the NFL," Perry said. "The information wasn't available to everybody like it is now. I was saddened because I thought I could make it in the NFL. I knew I had a chance and I felt like, 'Wow, all my opportunities are going down the drain.'"

Perry, of course, didn't give up. He tried to get fit for the postseason games, which included the Senior Bowl and the East-West Shrine game.

"In the East-West game on the other side was Walter Payton and Randy White, but I really couldn't play," Perry said.

But Perry's quickness, with his feet under him, was well known. A Raiders scout once clocked him at 4.3 in the 40, but told him years later he came in at 4.28.

"I knew I was fast but I didn't know I was that fast," Perry said. "He gave me a really good write-up."

Was the writing on the wall, though, when the 1975 draft sped through its first three rounds without Perry's name being called?

"The Raiders were disappointed when they saw me limping around after my senior season," Perry said. "I just didn't know what was going to happen and I talked a lot to my mom and dad about it. It was a very emotional time."

Perry's time came at No. 98 overall when he was selected by the Rams.

"When I got drafted I said, 'Lord, just let me get healthy,'" Perry pleaded. "But once we went up there for the minicamps, I still wasn't healthy. I had had the surgery in late February and the minicamps were in May. I was at about 60 percent, at best. But I think I showed them enough and they liked what they saw."

Perry's knee got right, but he contributed sparingly at first. He started just one game, before opening up eyes around the league when he intercepted eight passes in his second year.

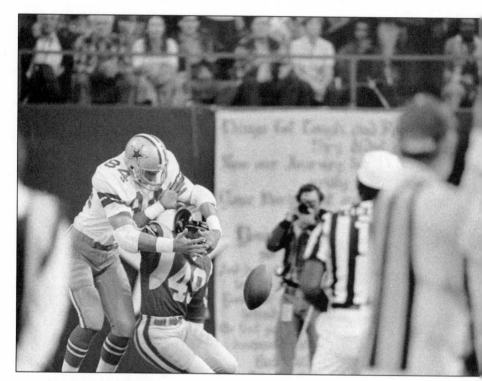

Perry was an integral part of one of the NFL's top secondaries during his time with the Rams. A two-time Pro Bowler, Perry had at least five interceptions for the Rams in three different seasons. (AP Photo/Bill Haber)

Perry would again battle injuries in his third year, but ultimately, the injuries lost out. Perry displayed the fortitude once more to overcome adversity and become a member of the Rams' 40th Anniversary Team.

"When I came into the NFL, I was damaged goods," Perry said. "But the Rams took a chance on me."

The Game

By Rod Perry

There are so many games, but the first game I think of is the one against the Dallas Cowboys in 1978. I was able to get two interceptions in the game and return one of them for a touchdown. I ended up being the Chevrolet NFL Player of the Week. And that was probably where my career really took off that year, too.

I had eight interceptions in 1976, but I was hurt in my third year. So in 1978 I came back and got eight interceptions and that day I got two against Dallas. That was a really fun game. I enjoyed it and I remember it.

The first interception we were in a Cover 2 where we had to read the coverage, something that [Rams defensive coordinator] Bud Carson brought in. If they put in backs you had to read that and if they put us in stacks. Bud was so far ahead of his time with coverage ideas.

I was on the weak side away from Tony Dorsett and Robert Newhouse. We jammed the receivers at the line and Tony Hill ran a curl. I slide inside of him and made the interception.

The second interception was in the fourth quarter and it was a bootleg and the boot was toward me on the outside. Tight end Billy Joe Dupree came off the line and went behind my back and I had someone in the flat and saw Roger Staubach look his way. I jumped in front of him and made the interception and turned upfield.

The fullback tried to tackle me but it I hurdled him and I cut in between Dorsett and someone else, I think one of their tackles. I took it in 43 yards and that was the final score, as we won 27-14.

That was a big-time play for me; it ended up having quite an impact on my career.

It's a great feeling when you get that ball in your hands and can take it into the end zone. I felt like I could score with that second one because I knew I had enough speed. If I could get my hands on it, I knew I could get it into the end zone. I got my hands on it, beat someone, and I headed for the sidelines.

You always think of making a catch like that. Then to have it come true, to have it happen, is unbelievable.

And with Roger being with the Cowboys I was going against one of the greatest quarterbacks at that time and who ever played. It was a great thrill to intercept him. I mean you're talking about someone who ended up being in the [Pro Football] Hall of Fame and one of the best to play in every category. I felt very good, very blessed, very happy to intercept him.

Also that was the national game of the week. Everyone was watching it on the East Coast and in the South.

The Cowboys had won the Super Bowl the year before and you know it was always going to come down to us and the Cowboys in the playoffs.

So to beat them was huge because they had beat us in 1975 in the NFC title game so it was nice to beat them in 1978.

And with the game being at the [Los Angeles Memorial] Coliseum it was just exciting and electric and I think it was a sellout. There were at least 80,000 people there. Any time you are playing in L.A. it's a big deal if you are a player. You get that feel in the stadium and it was buzzing prior to the game. My wife was in the stands and there was just this buzz like it had a playoff-type atmosphere with that type of game.

I always dreamed of playing in the Coliseum. I remember watching a game that was played there when I was young with my dad. It was the Dallas Cowboys and the Rams and I just said, "Wow," and I always wanted to play there.

I had visions of coming to UCLA so I could play there. So it was a dream come true that my first NFL score off a return would be in the Coliseum.

That season would be the first year I made the Pro Bowl. From that game against the Cowboys, I had now kind of come onto the scene. I had made a name for myself and the team was winning and playing well.

The Aftermath

It happens late in every NFL year, when the hype kicks into gear about that season's Super Bowl. The signature plays of past championship games are shown. Rod Perry is not sure, though, if he really needs to see it time and again.

"I'm not real fond of that clip," Perry said, although his disdain comes with a grin.

Perry can still feel the Terry Bradshaw pass that he nearly swatted away, the one aimed for John Stallworth in Super Bowl XIV. The Rams were playing in front of what was largely a home crowd of 103,985 at the Rose Bowl, they had the lead in the fourth quarter, and they were this close to punching a hole in the Steel Curtain.

Then Bradshaw showed his mettle in trying to fit a ball over Perry and into the speedy, but well-covered Stallworth's arms. Perry had a chance to knock it away and deflect the pass, which would go for a game-changing 73-yard touchdown.

"I really thought I had it," Perry said.

The meeting of those two elite athletes came at the Rams' 32-yardline in the fading light of Pasadena. While it's a football picture that is etched in the memories of Rams and Steelers fans, at closer inspection, it looks like a ballet photo. It's two people suspended in air, twisting their bodies in ways mere mortals couldn't.

"I really thought I was going to intercept that pass," Perry said. "But he jumped over the top of me and made the play. If I would have intercepted it, it would have been a different game."

If so, then maybe Super Bowl XIV is the game of Perry's life. Instead, it illustrates the highs and lows any football player must contend with.

The Rams had stymied the Steelers on the underneath routes when they turned to the long-ball attack.

"I remember listening to [Steelers coach] Chuck Noll later and he said they were going to take a deep shot because we were playing so close to the line of scrimmage," Perry said.

So Bradshaw, with good protection, winds up and spots Stallworth running even with Perry. Thinking he had help over the top, Perry cuts inside of Stallworth to make a play that he didn't make, and one that has been replayed in his head thousands of times.

"They ran a curl-and-go and I ran a close to him, I was right on his hip and I felt like I was in a good position to make a play," Perry said. "I was right on his hip and shoulder; I did everything right. But whenever we watch the play my son always says, 'Don't jump, Dad, don't jump!'"

Perry left his feet and when he landed, Stallworth had made a leaping snag in full stride. The lanky receiver was off to the end zone in pushing the Steelers ahead, 24–19, with 12 minutes remaining.

The Steelers would tack on one more touchdown as the Rams lost in their first Super Bowl appearance, 31–19.

"I really feel like Stallworth just made a great play," Perry said. "You had Stallworth catching the ball and Bradshaw putting just the right amount of arch on it to get it over me. I mean, those are two Hall of Fame players making an unbelievable play."

Years later Perry's path crossed with Donnie Shell, the ex-Steelers safety. He was familiar with the route as he tried to defend it numerous times when matched against Stallworth in workouts.

"He told me those guys worked on that play all the time in practice and it never worked," Perry said, and here comes that grin again. "But Bradshaw probably made the best throw he had ever made on it in the Super Bowl."

Perry doesn't hide from the fact he was on the wrong end of one of the greatest plays in Steelers history. In fact, he referred to that play as a secondary coach, usually with the visual help of the iconic picture, to instruct his players of what not to do.

"It was a great teaching moment about not leaving your feet and one I've used many times," Perry said. "Although it was a tough lesson to learn."

The play landed Perry and Stallworth on the cover of *Sports Illustrated* that week. Noted artist LeRoy Neiman did a painting of it and a print belongs to Perry.

"We just moved, so I've got to get it out of storage," Perry said.

A super disappointment didn't define Perry and he doesn't keep it packed away like a bitter man. Instead he's proud of how he competed against Bradshaw and Stallworth, two of the best to ever play their positions.

Chapter 8

JACK YOUNGBLOOD

Rams at Seahawks—November 4, 1979

BIRTH DATE:	January 26, 1950
HOMETOWN:	Jacksonville, Florida
RESIDENCE:	Orlando, Florida
JERSEY NO.:	85
POSITION:	Defensive end
HEIGHT:	6 foot 4
WEIGHT:	245 pounds

The Run-Up

Jack Youngblood, a guinea pig?

"That stuff was nasty," he said.

Youngblood was playing for the University of Florida while a newfangled concoction was being mixed on the sidelines. The liquid was invented to help spent Gators combat the oppressive Florida humidity, which often led to cramps.

The players were unanimous in chugging such a potion. Then the miracle juice floated across their lips.

"I didn't know what it was, but I knew it was horrible at first," Youngblood said.

But Youngblood and his teammates pinched their noses and ambled over to the No. 10 wash tub that held the punch, surrounded by chunks of ice.

"We didn't have a lot of paper cups so we took turns with a dipper," Youngblood said, swallowing hard as if he could still taste that sour beverage. "It was like we had a damn chuckwagon coming by and we would drink up."

The gig's up if you haven't guessed what Youngblood was sipping. It was Gatorade, but in its earliest stages.

"Dr. [Robert] Cade and Brady Greenhouse, our trainer, came up and said, 'Hey this stuff is a whole lot better than water,'" Youngblood said. "'It replenishes what you are sweating out with all its minerals.' I said, 'That sounds good to me.'"

Then he took a gulp.

"It tasted like crap," Youngblood said. "One day it would be too salty. The next day it was too sweet. Then it would be too thick or syrupy. One day it was like milk. But they kept mixing it up like a witches brew."

A larger-than-life figure with the Rams, Youngblood was known for his tenacity and his commitment. Youngblood really did play in Super Bowl XIV with a broken leg which added to his persona as Capt. Blood or as the John Wayne of the NFL.

Youngblood was a warlock at Florida no matter what he guzzled down his throat. Not only was he an All-America selection and ultimately enshrined in the College Football Hall of Fame, but to many, he was among the greatest players in Gators history.

Youngblood's ability to chase down quarterbacks and deny ball carriers additional yardage led to him being the Rams' first-round pick in 1971. Although it's doubtful, he toasted his selection with a glass of Gatorade.

"It did work," he said. "The science behind it made all the sense in the world. Because you were losing sodium and that deactivates the nerve endings. So you didn't have nearly the cramps you usually had after a hard workout when you drank it."

But the real task was stiff-arming the taste.

"It turned out they finally hit on it with that citrus flavor," Youngblood said. "They marketed it and it worked well for them.

"The bad part about it was we were the guinea pigs. For doing that, they should have given us at least one share of stock—there [were] only fifty of us.

"Just think about that. One share would have meant nothing to them. But if we could have had that one share we would all be as rich as Donald Trump by now."

Maybe that would eclipse the bad taste it left in Youngblood's mouth.

"Dr. Cade tried to kill us," Youngblood said with a laugh. "That first stuff was lethal."

The Game

By Jack Youngblood

I was kind of struggling in figuring out which one to really talk about. There are some you can remember to talk about, but for the most part, I had such a focus on the field that really all I remember is snap to snap.

The only thing you focused on was what was going on at that very moment. Sometimes you would remember what went on in the first quarter and you wouldn't remember the rest of the game until you saw it on film. I would watch the film and I would think, "I really did that? Who is that guy?"

But the game that stands out in my mind is the one where we set an NFL record. That was the Seattle game in 1979. We went up there and set several team records, with the most important one being we held them to minus-7 yards of total offense. And we shut them out, 24–0.

I chased Jim Zorn around the whole game. We had worked all week long [on] keeping him in the pocket. Because the little thing he would do is jump out of the pocket and run all over the field.

One time he scrambled after I pushed him out from the left side and Freddy Dryer got tied up with the double-team over on the other side. So we had let him out of the pocket.

Zorn was taking off down our sideline and I'm chasing him, too, behind Freddy. As I get to the sideline Freddy is standing there with his helmet off and he's screaming at coach [Ray] Malavasi. It's because Malavasi is screaming at Freddy.

Freddy was yelling, "Oh yeah? Then why don't you come out here and try to tackle him!"

There were some crazy moments over the years and that was one that always stands out. And it was a very good day for us as we shut them down completely; they had one first down. I think the longest play they had was for 14 yards. But we sacked Zorn six different times, which led to the minus-30 yards [passing]. And we shut down their running game [23 yards], too.

When you look at the numbers, it's hard to believe we did that.

They were trying to block me with a tackle and a tight end most of the time. And their running back would try to hit me whenever I got back to the pocket. But it didn't quite work out for them that day.

What I didn't like was that artificial turf in the Kingdome. I loved to run on it but I hated to fall down on it.

If you played back in our day, about half the teams we played had turf at that point. If we played on it early in the season, you had skinned knees and skinned elbows for the rest of the year. That stuff would eat your skin after you fell on it.

It was like painted concrete. Oh it had a little texture, but not enough to cushion your falls, that's for sure. Houston was the first one to have it and it was the worst one of them all.

In that Seattle game, we knew we were doing well. But we didn't have the numbers available to us, or the stats, on the sidelines. But we found out on the way home on the flight and we celebrated a little bit.

That's when you can finally catch your breath and realize you had a successful day. You sit back and replay the game in your head and some of the things that went on.

My experience was I didn't remember the good things; I remembered the bad things. I would remember when I got tied up with the linemen and didn't make a tackle I should have. Or when I missed because I took the wrong angle.

It's the errors that stood out in my head because I wanted to correct them for the next week and not do that again. Those mistakes stayed with you longer than the good plays.

But in that game I remember what Merlin Olsen always told me: "Focus on one snap at a time."

That was part of the learning curve I had to go through in my first year in 1971. Deacon Jones had injured his foot and I started four games at left end for him that year. And remember I had Merlin Olsen on my right wing, so if I screwed up he would kick my fanny.

It was his lesson that I used that day against Seattle. You take it one snap at a time and if you win each time, then that adds up over time.

That was exactly what I was thinking. It didn't matter if it was third and seven or whatever.

That game revealed the character Deacon and Merlin had and how they helped me. I have to give Merlin and Deacon all the credit.

When I was a rookie and trying to establish myself, Merlin and Deacon took a green kid from the University of Florida under their arm and showed me how to play the game. Both of them at one point and time in my first year, 1971, they individually came up to me and put their arms around my shoulder and said the same thing: "You can play, but we are going to teach you *how to play.*" That shows you what kind of men they were.

Man, I was all eyes and ears and said, "I'm all yours." Because I knew for a fact that I didn't have all the answers.

And those were huge shoes to fill when Deacon left in 1972.

I had Merlin for six years and that was awfully nice knowing I had a future Hall of Famer as my wing man.

Those two, Merlin and Deacon, were a great combo. I still have [the late] Merlin's email address and number in my phone.

And because of them, that helped us hold the Seahawks to minus-7 yards that day, and that's pretty good.

That record of minus-7 yards is one that is going to be hard to ever break. Especially how they move the football in today's world.

The Aftermath

Jack Youngblood had a diagnosis before Clarence Shields, the Rams' team doctor, had put his hands, or eyes, on Youngblood's left leg.

"It's broken, Doc," Youngblood told Shields.

The two were in the bowels of Texas Stadium, sent there in the second quarter, when Youngblood was injured. The Rams were battling their hated foe, the Dallas Cowboys, in a 1979 NFC divisional playoff game.

Youngblood, who had a career-high 18 sacks in his fifth All-Pro season, had had his leg twisted and now was trying to turn it over for Shields.

"In those days you would leave the field and go into the locker room," Youngblood said. "So we could take a picture of it. But I knew it was broken."

Shields wanted more proof than Youngblood's speculation. He put the damning X-rays up to the light, and the potential for the Rams' first Super Bowl bid began its descent into darkness.

"You've got a broken leg," Shields said.

What was starting to snap was Youngblood's patience.

"Dadgumit, I know I have a broken leg—I told you that," Youngblood barked at Shields. "Now tape it up because this is the divisional playoffs and we've got to go."

Shields revolted, much like many do at the thought of playing such a violent and physical game without two good legs to stand on.

While Youngblood pleaded for assistance, Shields stood his ground.

"I can't tape it up," he told Youngblood. "I just can't do that."

Was Shields upholding the oath written by Hippocrates, among the most revered documents a physician can lean on: to treat the ill to the best of one's ability?

Not sure Hippocrates thought of how that may play into a doctor absorbing the displeasure of one Herbert Jackson Youngblood III in the NFL's postseason.

"I can't tape it up," Shields repeated.

Youngblood's blood pressure was rising as he tried to figure a way to climb off that trainer's table. The veins in his neck protruded as he laid into Shields.

"Dadgumit Clarence, tape this dang thing up!" he shouted.

Shields felt the wrath but couldn't maneuver a wrap.

"Look Jack, I can't do it because I don't know how to tape it," Shields admitted.

Youngblood shooed him away like a horse does a pesky fly.

"'You mean you are a doctor and you don't know how to tape a leg?' We just laughed," Youngblood said, still howling to this day when telling the tale.

Then he turned serious and requested an audience with the Rams' assistant trainer.

"Go get [strength and conditioning coach] Garrett Giemont," Youngblood demanded. "He'll know how to do it."

Giemont was summoned and his instructions from Youngblood were clear: He'd be seeing stars unless he got Youngblood back out there to fight that dadgum foe with a star on its helmet.

"I wasn't doing it for my ego," Youngblood said. "I was doing it to help the team."

But first he had to convince coach Ray Malavasi that a man with a broken fibula could wrestle with the Cowboys' stout offensive line. Right tackle Rayfield Wright, a future Pro Football Hall of Famer, and right guard Tom Rafferty didn't give a hoot about a compromised Youngblood.

"Malavasi and the doctors trusted me," Youngblood said. "They knew I was not going to go out on that football field if it meant hurting our team. It was my duty to help the team the best I can."

Youngblood returned and the legend of him being the "John Wayne of the NFL" grew. Sure, Youngblood had taken a shot. But no way he was packing it in.

The Rams beat Roger Staubach—playing what turned out to be his final meaningful game—and the Cowboys, 21–19. Then they shut out the Tampa Bay Buccaneers, 9–0, the following week in the NFC Championship Game. Both teams had defeated the Rams during the regular season.

Youngblood kept playing, and that included Super Bowl XIV, where the Rams fell to the Pittsburgh Steelers, 31–19.

But the craziest part of the whole broken leg ordeal? Youngblood participated in the Pro Bowl as well one week after the Super Bowl.

The meaningless Pro Bowl, where the slightest of injuries caused players to wave off their inclusion?

"People would ask, 'Why did you play in the Pro Bowl?'" Youngblood said. "I said, 'Hell, if I can play with this leg in the playoffs I'm not going to miss the party in Hawaii.'"

Youngblood, even when there was not much more than a lei on the line, refused to lay down. And his legend as being among the NFL's toughest players was born.

Chapter 9

VINCE FERRAGAMO

Rams at Cowboys—December 30, 1979

BIRTH DATE:	April 24, 1954
HOMETOWN:	Torrance, California
RESIDENCE:	Orange Park Acres, California
JERSEY NO.:	15
POSITION:	Quarterback
HEIGHT:	6 foot 3
WEIGHT:	212 pounds

The Run-Up

Vince Ferragamo had that flowing Italian name and the University of Nebraska football pedigree.

But he was a kid who was raised on Southern California sports. He was born in Torrance and first started opening scouts' eyes with his big right arm at Wilmington's Banning High School, where one season he won the Los Angeles City Schools' Most Valuable Player Award.

"I was a local boy," he once told a group of Rams boosters.

That's why becoming a member of the Los Angeles Rams meant so much. And while the game of his life would come at Texas Stadium, Ferragamo always had a soft spot for the Los Angeles Memorial Coliseum. It was there that he absorbed the generations of memories it holds.

What other venue offers the mystique of hosting two Olympics, two Super Bowls, two major college teams, and where John F. Kennedy accepted the Democratic nomination to run for president in 1960?

Even Franklin D. Roosevelt took a lap around its storied track long before the Rams moved west from Cleveland after winning the 1945 NFL title.

"The Coliseum always had all those years of history," Ferragamo said. "What with the Rams being there, and USC and UCLA playing there on Saturdays when I played there years ago."

There's something about the Grand Old Lady built in 1923. Where else does your foot hit the turf and among the first things that is spotted is the Olympic cauldron, high above the venue's eastern flank?

"I remember coming out of the tunnel," Ferragamo said.

The fun, though, started before he laced up his cleats and made sure his game face was affixed just right. With South Central Los Angeles being a long Ferragamo pass from Tinsel Town, there were always pregame hijinks surrounding the Rams.

"Back in the locker rooms before our games the Hollywood personalities and comics would come in," he said. "It was fun to see them because they would be cracking jokes and it would lighten the whole atmosphere up."

Then the hangers-on would diminish and it would be just the players and coaches. At the appropriate time, the trek toward the turf would commence.

"You walk down the tunnel and hit the field and all the history in the Coliseum helps bring out the best in you," Ferragamo said. "There was that tradition and then you would look up and there would be 80,000 to 100,000 people cheering for you. It was pretty dramatic and it was exciting to run onto that field."

For the early parts of Ferragamo's Rams career, that was the highlight of the day. He didn't see much action behind starter Joe Namath, and then Pat Haden, trading his clipboard for the mop-up duties in his first two appearances in 1977.

They were hardly noteworthy, unless you're a kid from the South Bay and absorbing every moment of taking snaps at the Coliseum.

Ferragamo came in against the Minnesota Vikings on *Monday Night Football* with the Rams leading 35-3 and didn't throw a pass. His next cameo came when the Rams were annihilating the Tampa Bay Buccaneers, 31–0, and Ferragamo was a picture of perfection: one attempt good for one completion of 17 yards.

Only one quarterback directed the Los Angeles Rams to the Super Bowl and it was Ferragamo. He had to fight off numerous quarterbacks in securing the starting job during his Rams days, but no one was better in the team's 1979 playoff run.

He would see action in one more game, the last one of the season. At RFK Stadium against the Washington Redskins, Ferragamo threw two second-half touchdown passes to put the Rams in position for a win. But in ex-Rams coach George Allen's last game with the Redskins and in the NFL, Rafael Septien missed a game-winning field goal as time ran out.

Septien didn't get those critical three points and the team's three quarterbacks set off into a future mixed with success and failures.

Namath retired after being unable to withstand the game's physical requirements following the season's fourth game. He won two of his four starts, but his knees were shot.

Haden would claim Namath's starting spot, but with Ferragamo proving his worth, a juicy quarterback controversy would create numerous stories for the media corps.

Ferragamo, the kid from Torrance, was thrilled to be part of the team he grew up rooting for. No one knew he would lead the squad to its first Super Bowl in two seasons.

The Rams would head south down Interstate 5 just months after Super Bowl XIV, leaving the Coliseum in their rearview mirror, electing to share the Orange County city of Anaheim with the Angels and Disneyland.

But Ferragamo never forgot the unique way in which the Coliseum was, to him, the happiest place on Earth.

"It was a little bit of a different feel when we moved to Orange County," Ferragamo said about the team relocating in 1980, until moving to St. Louis in 1995. "We couldn't see the Hollywood Hills from Anaheim Stadium."

The Game

By Vince Ferragamo

With the Rams coming back to Los Angeles it brings the spirit and tradition back for the players, but the fans, too, remember. I still remember and they still remember.

They remember we were guys from the past and that they feel connected to. Like they were associated with us in some way. That was the way we played, too. We were a close-knit group. Everybody played for each other and not for themselves.

And of all the games I would have to pick the win over Dallas in the 1979 playoffs.

You have to remember when I took over the team—the Dallas game was my sixth start—we were just not a team that ran the ball exclusively. We would throw it if we had to throw it deep.

By throwing it deep we stretched the field and made the field tougher to cover. That made our running game a little easier to get going. And then we could make plays in the air.

I remember we did the same plays from the first day of training camp until into the Super Bowl. They were simplistic plays but we perfected them. We were so used to running the plays that we could run them against any defense.

In our offense most of the time if the quarterback read it right, there would be somebody open. If he didn't read it right, then something disastrous would happen. Thank God we had it the right way most of the time.

On that memorable touchdown pass against the Cowboys it was the 63 pattern, which is a combination of routes that they still run today in some fashion. We had Preston Dennard split out to the post and had Billy Waddy coming underneath to stretch the defense.

If they take away your short routes you go deep and if they cover you deep you go to the intermediate routes. That's where we had a shot.

Billy was coming across the middle and it was kind of a miracle that he caught the ball. They were in a prevent defense and rushed three guys. The pass was tipped by [linebacker] Mike Hegman.

But there was a hole in the coverage and Billy found that hole. The ball got there and he took it and started running across the field toward the sideline, then turned upfield and scored [a touchdown].

That put us ahead 21-19 with two minutes to play.

It was one of those miraculous things that happen. Maybe it isn't supposed to work but it did work and it was kind of magical in some ways.

But stuff like that happens when you go to a Super Bowl. You win games like that.

It is pretty neat still to see the video. It is a memory that won't ever be erased in your mind. It's like that for the players and the fans, too, that actually saw it because it was a special moment.

It's one of those big plays you remember.

Like Joe Montana's pass in the end zone to Dwight Clark, even though he's probably throwing the ball away.

Or that tipped pass when the Steelers won in the playoffs— The Immaculate Reception. Franco Harris wasn't ever supposed to be there. But he picked the ball up on a fluke play and ran into the end zone.

It happens so fast and a lot of that game against Dallas was a blur. But that's what happens in the NFL. The speed of the game is pretty fast and that's the best thing about it.

But on that play to Billy, you remember it every step of the way.

The Aftermath

The Rams rode that wave of postseason magic Ferragamo spoke of to Super Bowl XIV.

The following season, Ferragamo was even better, entrenched as the starter.

One year after he supplanted Pat Haden and led the Rams to the NFC title, he heaved a career-high 30 touchdown passes.

He went from having the game of his life in 1979 to the season of his life in 1980.

Ferragamo's big right arm had his career pointed in any direction not labeled "south."

Instead it went north: Ferragamo signed with the Canadian Football League as he said bonjour to the Montreal Alouettes.

But the rich contract in Canadian dollars ended up not making sense. Ferragamo's numbers didn't add up either as he went from being a splashy free-agent signing to an overpaid American riding the bench.

Then the Alouettes went toes up.

"I thought I had a pretty good deal," Ferragamo said at the time. "I never thought they would go bankrupt."

Then again Ferragamo never thought he would be playing 12-man football. It was only for a brief stint, as one year in the CFL was enough.

Ferragamo played three more years with the Rams. He had stints with Buffalo and Green Bay before retiring after the 1986 season.

He then stayed in the Orange County area, not far from his old Rams home, where the real estate business was as sweet to Ferragamo as fine wine.

In fact, Ferragamo now has his own vineyard and with a name like his, you can't be surprised he plopped some seeds in the ground in 2009.

"I started growing those grapes in Orange Acres," he told a Newport Beach Restaurant Week crowd. "To my surprise they started to proliferate. They started to grow really well. They can't grow as well as they do in Sicily, but they're still great."

Ferragamo, like his products, has aged well. He's even lived long enough to see the Rams mimic him: they moved away and then they returned.

"The Rams are back and we are so excited," he said. "When we were playing we had a connection with the fans. We were interactive with the fans. There's a lot of Rams fans where there's been a void."

Chapter 10

NOLAN CROMWELL

Rams at Buccaneers—September 11, 1980

BIRTH DATE:	January 30, 1955
HOMETOWN:	Smith Center, Kansas
RESIDENCE:	Canyon Lake, California
JERSEY NO.:	21
POSITION:	Safety
HEIGHT:	6 foot 1
WEIGHT:	201 pounds

The Run-Up

Nolan Cromwell was easy to find as a Kansas kid. Whatever sport was in season, one could locate the nimble Cromwell playing it.

"I'm not a big fan of one-sport athletes," Cromwell said. "I think you should play every sport you can. Basketball, track, even soccer, because it helps with the agility of your feet. I think if you limit yourself you are hurting your overall skills if you concentrate on football or basketball."

Cromwell was a track guy. A football guy. A basketball guy. If someone was keeping score, Cromwell had his body in the game. That's just how it was in the small town of Ransom, Kansas.

The Ransom Rambler? That would be Cromwell.

"Once football season was over it was the beginning of basketball practice," Cromwell said. "You would have the same guys on [the] team, all your buddies."

But it was Cromwell's siblings that honed his football skills that eventually led to him belonging to the NFL All-Decade Team of the 1980s as a Rams safety.

"I had some older brothers, four and eight years older, that pushed me and challenged me and it made my development as a young player a little quicker. So I was never afraid to guard a bigger guy than me.

"They would have their friends over and we would play football, basketball—whatever they were doing I would be doing it, too."

After two years at the University of Kansas, Cromwell was an All-Big 8 safety. But year three brought with it a new role for Cromwell.

"I was running track at the same time spring football was going on," Cromwell said. "I would do my track workout then run over and suit and go out and run drills in spring ball. Well after the first week coach [Bud] Moore called me over."

Moore was clear with his intent.

"I would like you to take a look at the quarterback position," Moore said.

Moore saw more than a safety in Cromwell. He spotted the perfect person to run his wishbone attack.

"It didn't matter to me," Cromwell said. "Whatever was best for the team."

Although it wasn't the best for Cromwell's health.

"I went over and ran the drills with the fullbacks, running the option," Cromwell said. "I was trying to get the steps down and I remember focusing so hard on how to read the defensive tackle. If he stepped one way, I would pull the ball away and go up field. If he stepped the other way, I would give it to the fullback."

Sounds good, but how did that work out?

"I was so focused on the tackle that I didn't see the defensive end," Cromwell said. "He hit me and I had the ball right in my chest. I remember the guy who hit me [during practice]. It was Tom Dinkel, who went on to play linebacker for the Bengals."

Cromwell might have had the eye of the tiger before the play. After it, he was seeing stars.

"You all right?" quarterback coach Gary Rutledge asked Cromwell.

He was, but Cromwell had learned a lesson that wasn't taught in the Kansas classrooms.

"I smiled and said, 'I should have pitched it,'" Cromwell said.

Rutledge nodded.

"Don't miss that read again," he said.

Cromwell didn't, just like he didn't long for playing safety.

"It was fun at quarterback and a good challenge," he said. "I got a chance to show more of my athleticism than I think I got to in high school."

Cromwell set a high standard. He became an honorable mention All-America quarterback on his way to a 1,000-yard rushing season as a junior. He led the Jayhawks to an upset win over then-No. 1 Oklahoma, which was the defending national champion.

True to his word, Cromwell didn't play football exclusively. He was an All-America selection in track and qualified for the Olympic Trials as a low hurdler.

The Game

By Nolan Cromwell

The interesting thing about the game of my life is I don't even remember it. It was probably the best quarter and a half of football I ever played when we lost to the Buccaneers, 10-9.

I intercepted a pass on a deep route, where I just went up and got it. When I was running it back a running back's foot hit me in the helmet and knocked me out halfway through the first quarter. I went to make a cut and someone dove from behind me and I tripped and was going down, [when] the running back comes flying in with a hit. It was a clean hit. No big deal.

After I got up, I didn't even remember anything that went on until just before halftime.

It happened about six, seven minutes into the first quarter and then the rest of first quarter and most [of] the second quarter.

I remember nothing until there are three seconds to go in the half when they line up for a field goal.

For the next quarter and [a] half, it was probably the best football that I had ever played. I watched the film and I was turning up on every play. I was covering the tight end. I was covering the deep middle.

Bud Carson was our defensive coordinator and he ended up going berserk on the sideline. We were not getting the checks in, which was my responsibility. I come off the field and [Carson] is hollering at me and I don't remember any of this until I see it on film.

I made a lot of the checks in our defense, based on Tampa Bay's formation, based on different things. There were certain Tampa Bay formations where we were supposed to check with everyone [on] what was going to happen. But I wasn't making checks so we just kept going. So no one was really playing what was called and it didn't matter. But we had a lot flexibility in our defense at the time so we were able to play.

But I don't know how I was playing. And I was telling everyone what I was going to do before every play. Some of the guys said, "He is out of it." But it was a great quarter and a half of football.

It was crazy that I was doing so well. You look at that film of me making the tackles and they were excellent tackles. I was squared up on people; my technique was pretty good.

Even the rest of the defensive backs were saying how good I was playing. They said, "You never tackle like that!" Everything was picture perfect.

The secondary was saying, "Don't worry about it. Keep playing that way."

It was at halftime that I finally came to after I didn't remember anything that went on.

But I was knocking people down, making tackles at the line of scrimmage. I was making plays that I wouldn't normally make, as I was just reading and reacting.

In the second half I could remember things at some point and I played the rest of the game. But with today's football and how they are treating concussions, which is a huge situation, I would not have had a chance for the game of my life.

The Aftermath

Nolan Cromwell played for the Rams from 1977 to 1987. That the competitive Cromwell stayed closed to the action after his playing days isn't surprising. A coaching career came calling and it didn't have to holler very loud.

Cromwell hung up his pads, then rekindled a dream he had held on to. Since he was in high school, Cromwell had been drawn to coaching. Rams head coach John Robinson invited Cromwell to join his staff in 1991.

Cromwell admits, though, he didn't have all the answers.

"I loved it so much," Cromwell said. "But to be very honest with you I was not a very good coach the first few years. You learn how to adjust, how to adapt."

The coaching carousel soon had Cromwell aboard. There were stops in Los Angeles, Green Bay, Seattle, St. Louis, and Cleveland. He directed special teams, worked with wide receivers, defense, and was even an offensive coordinator for Texas A&M.

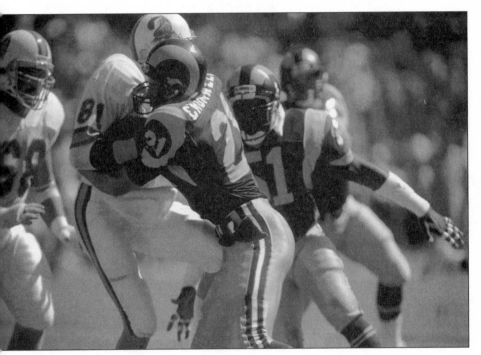

Cromwell was spectacular in monitoring the back end of the defense as his athletic skills allowed him to close quickly on receivers and deliver a stinging blow once he arrived.

"Growing up, I always wanted to coach," he said. "I was always looking forward to working with the younger kids.

"You got your guys and you teach them what you believe. Hopefully they grasp on to it and go out and perform."

His stint as the Packers' special teams coach, from 1992 to 1997, gave him a first-row seat to Green Bay's return to prominence. Green Bay won Super Bowl XXXI and it was a special teams player, Desmond Howard, who was named the game's MVP.

"I felt I could communicate pretty well with the players on the field," Cromwell said. "It was all about getting everyone focused and making sure they understood what their responsibilities were."

Unlike when Cromwell was cutting his teeth on the game, his players wanted to know the why as much as the when or the where.

"That was the biggest thing," Cromwell said. "They would ask, 'Why do I have to do it this way? Why do I have to do something when the quarterback is not looking my way?'"

What the players didn't know was what Cromwell did: A defensive play early in the game can be disguised and used later in the contest.

"Certain plays set up other plays," Cromwell said, repeating something he had told countless players. Just maybe where they are supposed to be on a play is setting someone else up.

Cromwell knew about being set up, even in his personal life. Otherwise, he might not have gotten married.

It was at a Rams luncheon when he spotted the then-Mary Lynne Gehr, a Rams cheerleader and a former Miss Hollywood.

"We talked briefly and that was that," Cromwell said.

But Cupid had fired a bow across Cromwell's grill. He followed up on Miss Gehr and it was a Hollywood story, where the star player gets the cheerleader.

Marriage and two kids followed and Cromwell is still grinning about the chain of events.

"That," Cromwell said quickly, "was the best thing that ever happened to me."

Chapter 11

JOHNNIE JOHNSON

Packers at Rams—September 21, 1980

BIRTHDATE:	October 8, 1956
HOMETOWN:	La Grange, Texas
RESIDENCE:	San Jose, California
JERSEY NO.:	20
POSITION:	Safety
HEIGHT:	6 foot 1
WEIGHT:	185 pounds

The Run-Up

The Rams were ecstatic in 1980 when a draft-day, first-round trade was consummated and they landed safety Johnnie Johnson, a Texas Longhorn standout.

Unfortunately, some Rams who were long in the tooth instituted a holdout upon learning what the team agreed to pay Johnson.

"It was actually one of the most difficult times in my life," Johnson said.

Johnson's dream of making the NFL was realized, it just didn't come with a Kumbaya feeling. When it came time to report to camp, the Rams' gang wasn't all there.

"I was so excited because I was going to play with Jack Young-blood, Jim Youngblood, Fred Dryer, all those guys," Johnson said. "But when I showed up for training camp they had all boycotted it because of the contract that I had signed. They were really hot."

Two years after Lee Majors had finished starring in *The Six Million Dollar Man*, Johnson was the Rams' $1 million man. They gave him that, plus $100,000, to be spread over six seasons—for the shocking sum of roughly $183,000 per year. Many Rams revolted.

"I was the highest paid defensive back in the NFL," Johnson said. "It was a big contract back then."

Ultimately, some Rams stars turned their back on the team. It was called the "Gone Fishin' Holdout" with the Youngbloods, Dennis Harrah, and Larry Brooks electing to wet their line instead of hooking up with their teammates.

Some of the players trickled back in. Others made a stand and weren't going to budge and blew off the preseason contests.

"The first time I saw Jack Youngblood, and I'll never forget this, was the Wednesday before the opening game against Detroit," Johnson said. "He didn't come to training camp in protest of the Rams giving me that contract. When I saw him I said, 'Thank God you finally got here.'"

Johnson had received his dough and other Rams, fresh off their first Super Bowl appearance, wanted management to spread the financial sugar around. They were ticked, as Johnson became the team's highest-paid player before even playing a snap.

But Johnson is quick to note those wanting to be compensated better never pointed a finger at him. There's an old adage in the NFL that Johnson was quickly learning. In pro football, everyone gets paid the same—which is whatever they can get.

"The players were really good about that," Johnson said. "Each one of the guys called me and said, 'Hey rookie, this has nothing to do against you. We're glad you got what you got. Our beef was with the Rams.' They made that very clear to me. But my big concern was just all this negative talk about me causing the holdouts."

Before Johnson would have the game of his life he was learning that life in the NFL was no game, but a business, and the Rams were eyeing the bottom line.

As a result of all the turmoil, Johnson had to watch which route he took to workouts each day so not to be cornered by the press. He was enemy No. 1 to many Rams fans, despite being the hometown team's No. 1 pick.

"I used to go to practice a different way every day trying to avoid the media," he said. "I just wanted to play football and prove myself. Everyone was asking, and the big question from the media was, 'Is he really worth that contract?'"

The team's No. 1 pick in 1980 got off on the wrong foot after signing a rich deal which made his future teammates jealous. But that was all forgotten once Johnson returned an interception for 99 yards and a touchdown in his rookie year. (AP Photo/Rod Boren)

It didn't take long for Johnson to supply the answer. Johnson, in the game of his life, returned an interception 99 yards for a touchdown in only his third appearance as a Ram in a decisive win over the Packers.

"After I intercepted that pass against Green Bay and ran it all the way back I will never forget Cullen Bryant running up and down our sideline," Johnson said. "He was saying, 'Is he worth it? Is he worth it?'

"I guess I had proven I was worth it."

The price was steep, but the Rams had gotten their man.

"I was their guy and they had indicated that to me," Johnson said. "When I didn't go to Green Bay with the sixth pick, the Rams traded with the Cleveland Browns to move up and draft me."

Johnson had been down about being the cause for so much commotion at training camp. But all was forgotten after Johnson's first interception earned him a place in the Rams' record book.

The Game

By Johnnie Johnson

We were picked to win the Super Bowl that year, but we lost our first two games. We lost at home to the Lions (41–20) and on the road on a Thursday night game to the Tampa Bay Buccaneers (10–9).

So going into the Packers game, that was a big game for us.

It was one of those games where everything went well for us offensively, we were making plays. Defensively, we played very well and we had four interceptions in the game and two of those were returned for touchdowns. We won, 51–21.

I had my very first NFL career interception in that game and I returned 99 yards for a touchdown. In fact, that is a Rams record that still stands. To get that early in your career and for it to still be standing today is something.

Before my return we had a combination coverage and it was a play-action pass. The tight end ran a crossing route and in that particular coverage I had the ability to come off of the tight and go outside to the No. 1 receiver.

[Packers quarterback] Lynn Dickey had some pressure on him and when he went to throw it, he got caught between going for the tight end or the No. 1 receiver.

I had the outside passing lane and when I caught it I took off and started thinking about my track and field days. That was exactly what ran through my mind. When I caught that pass and saw the sidelines, I headed toward it. Once I got behind a couple of the offensive players and into the open field, with my speed, I knew no one was going to catch me.

I think Dickey was caught in between, because of the pressure, of thinking he was going to throw it to the tight end and I would go to the wideout. But in the middle of the throw, he thought maybe to go back to the tight end—he just got caught in between what receiver he wanted to throw to because of such strong pressure. As a defensive back, I was always a big fan of quarterbacks being pressured.

I had lined up in the strong safety spot, right outside of the tight end. So if the tight end went out, I would cover him up top. I had underneath help from [Jim] Hacksaw Reynolds if he goes inside.

And we had help in the middle from safety Nolan Cromwell. We were passing off guys to each other in this combination man-zone coverage we were in.

It was early in the game, in the second quarter, when I got my interception, and that was a key play in the game when I think back. Because we had scored two touchdowns and a field goal; they had scored once and it was 17–7. But they were down in the red zone and if they would have scored they would have been back in the game, 17–14.

So not only they didn't score despite being in the red zone but we scored off the interception and that really just kind of turned the tide back into our favor. I remember [defensive coordinator] Bud Carson telling me how huge of a play that was.

What it does is put points on the board for you and it takes it off for them. When you bring it back 99 yards, it immediately puts points on the board and you do it without the offense ever taking the field. Doing that can really take the wind out of the sails of a team, when you really look at it.

It's much different than in basketball when you can have a breakaway and you don't score and they come down and score. That's a four-point turnaround, but that's just four points. In this instance it's a 14-point turnaround on one play. If they would have scored a touchdown it would have been a much different game at that time.

When I caught the ball, I was right on the goal line. But I guess one foot was on the 1-yard line, but [the return] could have easily been from the goal line for 100 yards.

We also had Pat Thomas at right corner and Rod Perry at left corner. Perry would intercept a ball for a touchdown for 83 yards that day as well. My interception kind of set the stage for Rod's later on because the Packers fell so far behind they had to start passing. It was a crazy number, getting four interceptions in one game. Rod had two and Pat had one.

They kept throwing it and it obviously wasn't working for them, which is why we had so many interceptions that day. That was one of the reasons why we were able to score 37 points in the second quarter.

Our secondary was pretty good. We were rated the No. 1 secondary in the NFL. That year all four of us made some team or another: All-Pro, Pro Bowl, rookie team. We all were listed as the top safeties and corners in the league.

I remember Vince [Ferragamo] had a good day and because we were so far ahead he didn't have to throw the ball much. He went 15 for 19 for three touchdowns.

We won that game to go on a five-game winning streak. That game launched us onto a winning run, where we won six of our next seven games.

The Aftermath

The Rams were in a pickle in 1989, so they turned to Johnnie Johnson. Never mind they hadn't protected him before the season despite him leading the squad with four interceptions in 1988.

Johnson, one of the most productive and popular Rams during his tenure, signed with the Seattle Seahawks before the 1989 season.

"That was the Plan B free agency and a team could protect only so many players," Johnson said. "They left me unprotected because they had a feeling that I was so loyal and committed to the Rams that I would be safe, that I would come back. I had business interests in the area and strong community ties and some thought I wouldn't leave."

But Seattle was enticing, even for a lifelong Ram. Chuck Knox, the former Rams coach, was leading the Seahawks. And Rod Perry, Johnson's old secondary pal, was coaching the defensive backs.

"But I wasn't looking forward to going up there and playing on that Astroturf," Johnson said, cognizant of what it did to aging knees. "But in talking to those guys I decided to give it a go."

Make that a give-and-go. Johnson gave the Seahawks three games, then bid them adieu.

"It almost killed me at that stage in my career," Johnson said. "When I started to play on it I thought, 'Oh no, this isn't going to work.' Chuck said, 'OK' and let me go. If it hadn't been for Chuck and Rod, I would have never gone there."

Johnson had already contemplated life after the NFL. He wanted to play for a decade and then move on to the next chapter in his life.

When the Seahawks invited him to the Great Pacific Northwest, that gave Johnson the opportunity for a tenth year in the NFL. But Johnson's creaky knees were telling him to call it a career.

So Johnson played those three games and went from back-pedaling into peddling houses. Then the phone rang at his ERA All-Pro Real Estate office and the call was coming from a familiar area code. The Rams were getting ready to face the San Francisco 49ers in the 1989 NFC Championship Game and their secondary depth had been shredded.

Vincent Newsome and Darryl Henley had been injured the previous week in the overtime win versus the New York Giants. They joined ailing defensive backs Anthony Newman and Clifford Hicks already on the sidelines.

The desperate Rams scratched their head until someone suggested dialing Johnson. It was an interesting idea, but Johnson was consumed doing other things.

"At least he's well rested," Rams coach John Robinson said at the time. "Our biggest problem is that he sells real estate, and he has an open house Sunday."

But Johnson was more concerned about completing a real estate deal than making sure Joe Montana didn't complete a pass.

"When they originally called I said I had no interest in returning," Johnson said. "I really had no interest, but they kept calling. They were saying, 'There's no one that knows our system as well as you do so it won't take you long to come in and get up to speed. This is a real need that we have.'"

Johnson didn't have the gumption to decline. His old club was in dire straits and just maybe Johnson could straighten them out and get to the Super Bowl that he missed by one year when starting his career.

"The year before I got here, the Rams got to the Super Bowl," he said. "If they'd have gone the year after I left, I don't know if that would have settled with me."

So Johnson packed a bag and headed back to the Rams' facility.

"Once a Ram," Johnson said. "Always a Ram."

Johnson, then 33, strapped the pads back on. Well past the game of his life during his rookie season, he hoped to contribute in one more game to extend his NFL life.

"I had kept myself in good shape by playing tennis," Johnson said.

But after the 49ers thumped the Rams, 30–3, it was game, set, and match for Johnson as far as his NFL days were concerned.

"I did play in that game and yeah it was the championship game which they won rather handily," Johnson said. "But just like in that game of my life against Green Bay, there were a couple of plays early in the game that made the difference.

"Flipper Anderson came wide open deep on a play-action and if we would have completed that pass we would have gone up 10-0. They were in some kind of a Cover 2 coverage and Ronnie Lott came all the way over from the opposite side of the field to knock the pass away.

"After that the whole flow of the game changed because we had to give the ball back to them. Then they started to hit some plays and we never recovered."

Chapter 12

LEROY IRVIN

Rams at Falcons—October 11, 1981

BIRTH DATE:	September 15, 1957
HOMETOWN:	Fort Dix, New Jersey
RESIDENCE:	Anaheim Hills, California
JERSEY NO.:	47
POSITION:	Cornerback/punt returner
HEIGHT:	5 foot 11
WEIGHT:	184 pounds

The Run-Up

LeRoy Irvin etched his name in the NFL record book as a punt returner. But despite the 207 yards he collected on six punt returns against the Atlanta Falcons on October 11, 1981, don't overlook his prowess as a defensive back.

Irvin is among a handful of NFL players to be selected to the All-Pro team at two different positions. For Irvin, those spots were as a returner and a cornerback.

At the University of Kansas, Irvin was something special in the Jayhawks' secondary.

He was the only freshman starter in 1976, the same year future Rams teammate and fellow defensive back Nolan Cromwell was a senior and the team's starting quarterback.

As a sophomore, Irvin had 106 tackles, including 15 against UCLA.

His junior season saw him lead the team with 127 tackles.

As a senior, he notched 21 tackles in a game vs. Missouri.

Irvin considered himself as a cornerback first and a returner second. But when he joined the Rams as a third-round pick in 1980, his pass defense played second fiddle to him snatching punts from the sky.

Two Pro Bowl corners, Pat Thomas and Rod Perry, clogged Irvin's path to the Rams' starting lineup.

"I was backing up Thomas," Irvin said.

The next year Thomas and Perry would combine for seven interceptions, keeping Irvin on the bench. But Irvin kept his ears open and his nose to the grindstone.

"I listened to everything Rod Perry and Pat Thomas told me," Irvin said. "I really admired how they would talk to me and give me pointers. Because back then we weren't making that much money and I was trying to take their job. I just tried to go out and emulate what they did."

But Irvin was on the second team again in 1982. It was after that season that the Rams made a switch.

Jack Faulkner in the Rams personnel department was eager to take the secondary in a younger direction.

"Jack Faulkner, God rest his soul, he believed in me," Irvin said. "No way I was going to take Rod and Pat's jobs from them early on and I didn't dare think I was going to do that. But I knew that offseason that something was in the works. When those guys weren't there, I knew I had a shot at starting.

"But it was bittersweet. Because those two guys had taken me under their wing and taught me the game. They knew I was there to take their job, but they unselfishly gave me the knowledge and information to do that. I'm still friends with those guys to this day."

Irvin, in his first year running with the first unit, produced four interceptions (tying him for the team high), two fumble recoveries, and a sack.

It took patience but Irvin, a member of the Kansas University Athletics Hall of Fame, had established himself as an NFL starting cornerback. In 1985 and '86, he was named All-Pro. In 1981 and '82, he had earned the same distinction as a punt returner.

Irvin said his mind-set as a punt returner helped him shut down the game's best receivers of the day.

"You can't be nervous," he added. "And you have to be fearless in your heart."

Irvin was one smooth returner and he proved it in the game of his life. His skill-set was transferable to another position, which

Irvin (47) was a dynamite cornerback, but some forget just how shifty he was as a punt-returner. His record of returning two punts for touchdowns in the same contest still stands and figures to be among the toughest to tie, let alone break in the game. (AP Photo/Bob Galbraith)

led to him being among the most prolific cornerbacks in Rams history.

The Game

By LeRoy Irvin

It has to be the game where I broke the record for punt-return yards in 1981 in Atlanta, when we beat the Falcons, 37–35. I grew up in Augusta, so it was a homecoming for me. And it was the first NFL game my dad ever came to.

But it was a crazy game because we went out the night before and broke curfew. We got in late and I was really tired that day, but the adrenaline kicked in.

The night before we went to the Limelight Club in Buckhead, Georgia, and a couple other bars. Back then the clubs didn't close until 4:00 a.m., but we got in around 1:00 or 2:00. But it still made for a short night.

I was starting at corner that week, too, so it was a very eventful game for me.

What happened was in the first quarter they punted it to me and I returned it 75 yards for a touchdown. Then in the fourth quarter, they punted it to me again.

Now that was crazy that they would punt it to me again, but the Falcons coaches were so arrogant that they thought they could punt it to me and I would not return it.

So the one in the second half I returned 84 yards for another touchdown.

I just don't think nowadays that would happen. When you are hot or a great punt returner, you are lucky if you get one return for a touchdown. Instead they punt it away from you if they know you are hot.

But the Falcons punted to me again and that just threw fuel on the fire. That's why I don't think the yardage record will ever be broken, because teams won't punt to the guy. It's lasted since 1981; it's already been a long time.

My only regret was on the third punt return I brought it back 45 yards and I actually just ran out of bounds. I was tired from getting in so late the night before and I was starting at cornerback.

But it goes back to the night before. I guess I was still on L.A. time. But if I would have stayed in, that would have given me some extra juice to take the record to a place where it might never be broken.

One coach did see me come in that night and he kind of kept it to himself all these years. Linebackers coach [Herb] Paterra did see me walking in and I still thank him to this day. Or maybe he didn't know I was coming in, but it was pretty early in the morning.

On those punt returns, I made a bunch of moves and we had some great special teams players. Back then guys would make a career out of special teams. I had guys like Reggie Doss, Joe Harris, Jimmy Collins, Lucious Smith, and Kirk Collins. It was a very special day.

My dad was very, very excited and very proud.

The Aftermath

LeRoy Irvin undoubtedly displayed his dance moves, when out clubbing the night before the game of his life. Just maybe that served him well in 1986 for the "Let's Ram It" video.

"Remember the Chicago Bears had their video the year before," Irvin said. "We were going to play them on Monday night that week when we did the video."

So the Rams followed suit with their version, even if some guys had some challenges following the choreographed scenes.

"We had so much fun and we danced," said Jackie Slater, Irvin's teammate. "And we found out who couldn't dance."

Everyone knows return men and cornerbacks have fluid hips, so Irvin was put on the front line. He was stationed two down from Nolan Cromwell and next to Eric "Top Gun" Dickerson. Irvin was waving his arms and shimmying, a mixture of Mr. Bojangles and Fred Astaire.

Irvin had one of the big parts at the video's 3.45 mark, when the camera zoomed in and he started rapping: "The Iceman cometh and Leroy's the name. I cover the corner, interceptions are my game. I score more than anybody else on the 'D' because I move like a cat, as you can see."

The video is a hoot to watch, an enjoyable voyage back into the Rams' time machine.

"I had never danced before," said Cromwell, who was called "Hollywood Handsome." "The things you do when you are young always come back to haunt you."

Maybe "Big Bad Jackie" Slater was talking about Cromwell and others, with this line:

"We can't sing and our dancing's not pretty, but we'll do our best for the team and the city."

Irvin mentioned Cromwell and Carl Ekern for being among the players with all the wrong moves.

Yet the video is priceless.

"That video is out there forever on YouTube," Irvin said.

It's etched in Rams lore, complete with the Embraceable Ewes moving and shaking with their mid-1980s hair fashions. Funny that after all these years, the chorus rings true with the Rams returning to L.A. in 2015 from St. Louis.

"We'll be rockin' L.A. so let's ram it today."

Chapter 13

DENNIS HARRAH

Rams at Jets—September 25, 1983

BIRTH DATE:	March 9, 1953
HOMETOWN:	Charleston, West Virginia
RESIDENCE:	Paso Robles, California
JERSEY NO.:	60
POSITION:	Guard
HEIGHT:	6 foot 5
WEIGHT:	260 pounds

The Run-Up

The 1979 Rams, yes the 9–7 Rams, were heading to Super Bowl XIV. And one Dennis Wayne Harrah wanted to arrive in style when facing the Pittsburgh Steelers at the Rose Bowl for the NFL title.

"I had rented a Rolls-Royce to drive to the game," said Harrah, and anyone who knew him wasn't surprised.

But when one cruises in a Rolls-Royce and is a key member of a Super Bowl team, that ride can't be stashed with commoners. Instead, Harrah was bent on obtaining preferred parking to show off his wheels and not to tax himself by making the long hike from a distant parking lot in the Arroyo Seco.

"I was worried more about getting a parking pass than fighting 'Mean' Joe Greene," he said, with his laugh that doesn't eclipse his southern drawl. "I was just 25 years old and thinking I will be back to the Super Bowl again. I was young and not very smart at the time."

Instead of fretting about neutralizing the Steel Curtain, Harrah wondered how to get around the wood sawhorses into the VIP lot.

In the days before the game, Harrah's request was repeatedly turned down. Harrah played one last card when he reached out to Don Klosterman, the Rams' general manager.

"I finally had to go to Don and get a parking pass for the Rolls-Royce," Harrah said.

But Klosterman was worried word would leak about Harrah getting special treatment.

"I couldn't tell anyone about the parking pass, is what Don told me," Harrah said. "Here I was getting ready to play in a game in which we would earn like $18,000 if we won and I'm more worried about not being able to get a parking pass than playing in the game.

"When you are 25 years old, it's just hard to have a sense of reality. It was for me anyway."

Harrah was young, and he questioned the old-school ways of coach Ray Malavasi leading up to Super Bowl XIV.

"We practiced hard for two weeks before the Super Bowl," Harrah said. "We were scrimmaging and beating each other up before the battle. I always wondered why you practiced so hard; that never made any sense to me. Ray made us beat each other up for two weeks."

Come game day, Harrah had some world-beaters across the line in Greene and Jack Lambert.

"I just used to love to play against them," Harrah said. "I would hold Lambert and he would cuss me out. He would be yelling, 'F this, F that.' But he had no front teeth, so spit would be flying from every direction. It was just a wonderful time.

"The main thing about playing 'Mean' Joe Greene was that if you held him, you didn't hold him too long. The last thing you wanted to do was to make 'Mean' Joe Greene mad. I did some things that I probably shouldn't have done to him, but I remember that I didn't do them for long."

It was during that game that Coca-Cola aired its classic commercial, which first aired in 1979, where Greene flips an appreciative kid his jersey.

Harrah never got a Coke or a smile that day, but he did get his parking pass.

The Steelers rallied for a 31-19 win in Super Bowl XIV. The Rams led at halftime (13-10) and after three quarters (19-17) but they couldn't stymie the Steelers' passing attack over the final 15 minutes.

"Needless to say it was a great battle," Harrah said. "I just wish we could have stopped the game after the third quarter."

If they had, Harrah would have driven home in style, as a winner.

The Game

By Dennis Harrah

It's hard to pick just one game, but the one that jumped out for me was against the New York Jets. That was the game that I definitely remember because it had probably the greatest fight of all times. It was definitely a battle at Shea Stadium.

I can remember very little of the Super Bowl and the Pro Bowls. But that one game, the one in New York, it was a great day.

I remember it the most because it meant so much to me. I enjoyed that game more than any other one. And it was because of a fight.

Did we win? I don't know if I remember [the Rams lost 27-24 in overtime]. All I remember is that fight.

The main thing was we all talked before the game and said if Mark Gastineau got a sack and started doing his dance and all that other stuff, we were going to take him out.

Well, Mark got around Jackie Slater, and needless to say he started doing his dance.

I think it was around the third quarter, somewhere later in the game. Jackie and the line had held him out pretty well. The line was doing well. But it was just one of those things that happen during the game.

When it happened I was battling Joe Klecko and I was so tired. I looked over and was waiting to see if Jackie was going to go after Mark. When Jackie started to go after him I said, "Hell, now I got to go over there now."

So I put my head down and I'm going to ram him. But right when I got there Mark sidestepped me and clubbed me in the head. He drove my face right into the ground.

It wasn't the fact that I wasn't willing to fight, it was just I was a little out of control as usual.

I think we had 11 guys at one time piling on him and to be honest with you, I got knocked down three times. I was one of the only guys that got in the fight and didn't get fined. The NFL must have felt sorry for me.

Finally, at the end of the fight I got to Gastineau and I punched him in the gut. That was my claim to fame, although it took two other guys to hold him.

So everybody gets fined and I didn't, so they all made fun of me.

We had 21 guys get fined $8,450. They had 16 players fined $7,300.

Needless to say it was a lot of fun. Yep, that was one of the greatest fights that I was ever involved in.

Super Bowl XIV probably should have been the greatest game that I had ever participated in. But that game [against the Jets], that fight, made it the one I remember the most.

The Aftermath

Dennis Harrah was "Bird Legs" to Tom Mack. The Rams legend and future Hall of Famer used to needle the young Harrah with joy.

Harrah didn't mind people poking fun at his physique or his West Virginia drawl. It was all part of the price to pay to be a Ram, and few players embraced that role more than Harrah.

"We gave him a hard time about those bird legs of his," Mack said.

Harrah had a comeback, it just wasn't a very good one.

"I've done squats until I'm blue in the face and I can't get my legs bigger," he said.

Mack was taking Harrah, whose career was just taking flight in 1976, under his wing. Harrah, who struggled in his rookie year, just didn't know it.

"He was a bona fide jerk at all times, but he was a jerk with nothing but fun in his heart," Harrah said. "There was no malice about Tom. He was the first man to come over and help you out of a situation, on the field and off."

It was a gesture by Harrah in Mack's final game that will long be remembered in Rams lore. During the 1979 Pro Bowl game at the Los Angeles Memorial Coliseum, reality boomed over the speakers from the game announcer to the crowd. Mack, the heart-and-soul of the Rams, was playing in his last game.

Harrah, who was on the field, held his hand high in the air. He signaled for the man who teased him like a little brother to return to the huddle. Mack ambled back out showered in a standing ovation and then shook hands with each member of the NFC and AFC teams.

"I was just thankful my dumb butt thought of it at the time," Harrah said.

Many remember him being a free spirit, especially those who hung out with him at his watering hole, Legends, in Belmont Shores.

Harrah, a six-time Pro Bowler, never lost his West Virginia twang or his ability to send defenders in the direction Harrah wanted. The longtime Rams captain didn't take any gruff from anyone and distributed it to everyone. (AP Photo/ Ray Stubblebine)

"Those days were fun, of what I remember," he said, with a chuckle. "They are a little blurry."

What was crystal clear was that Harrah was a leader and the proud captain of the Rams for six seasons. The six-time Pro Bowler started for 12 years, never looking for the easy way out.

But in 1987 his back revolted. A herniated disk was causing unbearable pain, almost as much hurt as Harrah felt when walking out to midfield for the post game handshakes.

"I didn't know anybody anymore, the guys that I had grown up playing with were all gone," he said. "So I quit walking across the field.

"I remember sitting in the locker room with Doug Smith in my last year and I didn't know some of the guys' names. That's pretty bad when you don't know your teammates' names, so I figured it was about time for me to leave."

It was last call for Harrah, but before settling up, he took with him a vault full of memories. He played in Super Bowl XIV and he had the game of his life in that donnybrook in Queens. But what made him feel like he was king for a day was when the Los Angeles Rams invited him back in 2016.

"I got to light the torch [at the Coliseum] for the game against the 49ers," he said, the big tough guy again showing his softer side. "I got to take my two sons and my wife and it was the first time I got to take my boys to a Rams game. I was so blessed to be able to do that."

Harrah felt back at home, a sensation he didn't get when Rams alumni were honored in St. Louis. Despite the credentials of the team's all-time greats, the Missouri faithful didn't appreciate their significance.

It was of no fault of the St. Louis Rams fans, as they didn't comprehend what Harrah, and others, once meant to the franchise.

"That was sort of the way it was in St. Louis," Harrah said.

But not so in Los Angeles, as Harrah's name still solicits cheers and smiles.

"The Rams, and Coach [Jeff] Fisher, wanted to bring us back to be part of it again," Harrah said. "It just didn't feel right in St. Louis."

When Harrah got to bring the iconic L.A. Memorial Coliseum torch to life, it might have trumped that day in Shea Stadium when he had the game of his life.

"I was so blessed to be able to do that, and that is probably one of the highlights of my life," Harrah said. "To light the torch and to have my sons on the sidelines was just a fantastic moment."

Old "Bird Legs" was flying high.

Chapter 14

MIKE LANSFORD

Rams at Saints—December 18, 1983

BIRTH DATE:	July 20, 1958
HOMETOWN:	Arcadia, California
RESIDENCE:	Tustin, California
JERSEY NO.:	1
POSITION:	Kicker
HEIGHT:	6 feet
WEIGHT:	183 pounds

The Run-Up

Mike Lansford was staying with his parents after three NFL teams booted him to the curb. The former can't-miss kicker from Washington was doing the opposite at that time—he was missing.

This was true while he was with the Giants for a New York minute in 1980.

"I couldn't kick the NFL ball," Lansford said. "Bill Belichick was my special teams coach and he is looking around thinking, 'What are we doing drafting this guy?' That was back when there were 12 rounds and I was a 12th-round pick."

Lansford's problem was lifting the football off the ground. The tee he used in college, which elevates the football, wasn't legal.

"I couldn't get under the ball," Lansford said, still sounding amazed.

What was alarming were his scattering kicks. The leg that had helped Pasadena City College to the final Junior Rose Bowl victory in 1977 and set a Pac-10 record at the University of Washington was absent.

"I had used the 2-inch tee at Washington, the biggest one they had," he said. "I know that doesn't sound like much but when it wasn't there it was affecting my kicks. It's like a golfer hitting a ball off a tee instead of hitting it off the ground."

Yet Lansford couldn't find a window of opportunity because he was repeatedly being shown the door.

After the Giants released him, the 49ers learned there was no gold in Lansford. The Raiders had the same response after Lansford's tryout.

Undaunted, Lansford kept kicking while he stayed at his parents' Arcadia home. Years after being drafted Lansford was tinkering with his craft.

"I was still trying to figure it out," he said. "I didn't want to work for a living and I believed I was pretty good at it."

He proved his worth, thanks to his irritated right foot.

"I was getting ready to kick one day and that morning when I was putting on my cleats my heel felt raw," Lansford said. "There was a blister on my right foot."

Lansford ditched his right shoe and his inaccurate ways rode along. No longer encumbered by a shoe, Lansford met the ball in a pristine manner.

Visions of Tony Franklin, the Eagles' barefoot kicker, raced through Lansford's head.

"He was kicking the [stuff] out of the ball and I thought, 'If he is doing it why don't I try it?' " Lansford said. "With the first kick I knew something was different. By removing the cleat it dropped the sole of my foot down lower. It was like hitting a sand wedge."

So a resurrected Lansford starting pitching his services to the NFL. But his calling card needed work.

"Yeah, remember me, the guy you cut two years ago?" he said. "I'm back and now I don't wear a shoe."

Rams executive Jack Faulkner bit, but only after George Strugar rang. The former Rams and University of Washington player called on Lansford's behalf.

Faulkner invited Lansford to audition before the strike-shortened 1982 season.

Frank Corral, the Rams' returning kicker and punter, was coming off a challenging year. When he reported to camp at not his physical peak, Lansford pounced.

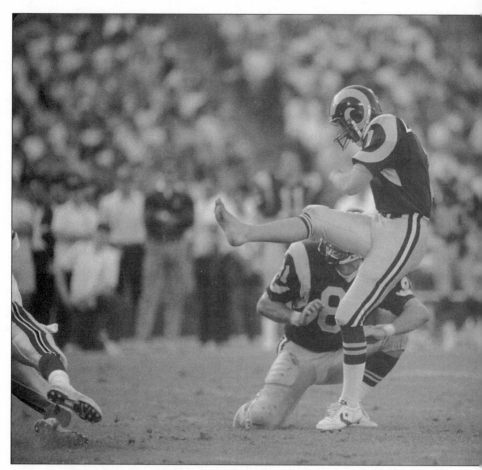

If the shoe fits, it must not belong to Lansford. The bare-footed kicker not only was unique in using but one cleat but also with his clutch performances. His aim was true, and the same goes for then-owner Georgia Frontiere, when she planted kisses on her favorite kicker.

"He couldn't quite keep up," Lansford said. "And I made the team."

He did all right under Ray Malavasi, but Lansford would have to impress a new coach the following season. The Rams canned Malavasi and hired USC's John Robinson.

Lansford had an opportunity after Chuck Nelson, drafted out of Washington and the Rams kicker, injured his back late in the season.

That led weeks later to Lansford's game of his life.

Lansford would forge a nine-year career, which included seven game-winning kicks. In fact, Lansford never missed in the final minute of regulation, or in overtime, when attempting a go-ahead or tying field goal.

When you follow a clutch kicker like the barefooted Lansford, it only means one thing: His is a big shoe to fill.

The Game

By Mike Lansford

It was the last game of the regular season against the Saints and we're down in New Orleans. Both of us are 8–7. But they had never been to the playoffs and we didn't go the previous year.

Plus it was Eric Dickerson's first year—this game was a big deal.

We scored on a safety, a punt return, and two interception returns for touchdowns. Despite all of that we are still down, 24–23, with two seconds left.

We got the ball back and I knocked down the kick. Based on that kick, that put us in the playoffs and it cemented my place with the team. That kick secured my position with [coach] John Robinson and the Rams.

Before the season, which was Robinson's first with the Rams, he brings in every USC guy that he knows at kicker, as well as all the Pac-10 kickers he went against when coaching USC.

Chuck Nelson was selected in the fourth round and I had kicked ahead of him at the University of Washington. So that was very awkward for him to be brought in to take my place. Not because he was a bad guy. It was just the previous year he had beat Robinson at USC. So that was what Robinson knew.

Well Chuck hurts his back with four games remaining, so I end up as the kicker.

In New Orleans that day, it's late in the game and they could have kicked a 52-yard field goal that would have put them up by five points. And they had Morten Anderson, the best kicker I had ever seen. I was thinking he could certainly put the game out of reach. But they punted.

Vince Ferragamo hits Preston Dennard a couple of times on passes and we are getting toward midfield. I started thinking I might have a chance at a kick.

I did a good job of staying away from people. They would come up and say something and it would make me nervous. Instead I tried to do my best to focus on the things I needed to focus on in my mind and not just be freaking out.

The kick was from 42 yards with time running out and I thought I was going to [soil] my pants. This was my big chance and my teeth were chattering.

The crowd was so loud that you had to put your hands over the ear holes in your helmets to hear anything. It was just deafening and it scared the [crap] out of me.

To tell you the truth I was lucky to make it.

Doug Barnett was the regular long snapper and was in his second year of doing it. But he hurt his knee in the first quarter and Doug Smith, our starting center, took his place. Smith had sure hands, but he had been playing center the whole game.

The snap was high and Nolan Cromwell pulled it off his left ear. Once I saw that it was a bad snap, something clicked in me and I was no longer nervous. It was like it allowed me to slow down and come through the ball. And Nolan is such a great athlete with great hands that he was able to pull it off.

I pulled it left of center and it kept drifting that way. It sneaked inside the left upright and it was all so surreal.

I was out of my mind; my heart was pounding so hard. I had never done anything close to this. I had never had a game-winner.

It showed, too, that I was an NFL kicker and relieved all doubt in John Robinson's mind and with the Rams. It gave them the confidence in me and I just continued to improve and get better and better and better.

And from that point on, I was known for being able to kick under pressure.

The Aftermath

Following the kick from the game of his life, Mike Lansford could hardly contain himself. He leaped high off the ground, while puncturing the air with his exuberant right fist. If he wasn't mobbed immediately by teammates hugging him, he might have run and kissed someone.

Which reminds Lansford of another story when someone gave him a big smooch.

"She called it giving some 'sugar,'" Lansford said.

She is "Madame Ram," former Rams owner Georgia Frontiere. To say the former lounge singer wasn't keen on the finer points of football would be as spot-on as Lansford's game-winning kick in New Orleans.

"She was clueless, nuts . . . a real beauty," Lansford said, not with ridicule but with a knowing chuckle. "She would bring her Hollywood friends around to entertain us—once she brought an opera singer. She was someone who had had nothing to do with sports and she couldn't relate to the players."

That didn't stop her from being a pregame presence on the sidelines. But instead of being like most owners and patting a player on the backside to wish him good luck, Frontiere would pucker up those lips caked in bright red lipstick.

"I went to go give her a high-five before a game and she gave me some 'sugar,'" Lansford said. "And she really planted one on me."

Lansford absorbed the smooch on his cheek, tugged back on his helmet, and jogged out on the field.

"We were playing the Chargers and this very big lineman looked over my way," Lansford said. "He yells, 'Hey kicker,' and wipes his cheek with his hand."

Lansford got the message, knowing Frontiere had made her mark.

"There was a big glob of lipstick on my face," Lansford said. "So I'm on the field wiping it off, but it won't all come off. I played the game with the lipstick on my cheek. That was something I will never forget."

Frontiere had a way of producing memorable moments. Those riding the team bus to RFK Stadium to play the Washington Redskins on January 1, 1984, in an NFC Divisional Playoff game just a few weeks after Lansford's game of his life, remember another Frontiere fumble.

"She would always give us gifts around Christmastime," Lansford said. "This year she did it when we were on the road, the night before we are playing the defending Super Bowl champions. That was the year Cabbage Patch dolls were the rage, the big collectable toy item. They were really a big deal."

Frontiere thought likewise, and you guessed it, bought each of her big, strong football players a doll. But with them being away from home, they couldn't stash the present in their locker or car.

Instead, when they reached the RFK parking lot and disbarred from the bus, they all did so with a Cabbage Patch doll under their wing.

"We are holding these things like a bunch of morons," Lansford said. "The Redskins fans in the lot let us have it. That was back when they had the Hogs and the Smurfs and they are all dancing around laughing at us and pointing to our Cabbage Patch dolls."

Those dolls brought little luck to the outclassed Rams.

"We walk into the stadium and soon after the Redskins destroy us," Lansford said. "It was 38–7 at halftime and they go on to win 51-7. It was bad. They just killed us."

At least the players knew a cuddly doll awaited each of them once they peeled off their pads.

"So now when we leave the stadium after getting destroyed, we all have to walk out with our dolls," Lansford said. "It felt about as demeaning and embarrassing as you could be."

Chapter 15

ERIC DICKERSON

Cowboys at Rams—January 4, 1986

BIRTH DATE:	September 2, 1960
RESIDENCE:	Los Angeles, California
HOME TOWN:	Sealy, Texas
JERSEY NO.:	29
POSITION:	Running back
HEIGHT:	6 foot 3
WEIGHT:	220 pounds

The Run-Up

Eric Dickerson's emergence in the NFL wasn't real subtle. It was similar to the way in which one of his high-stepping, powerful legs would sometimes pop a defender in the mouth.

Dickerson, nicknamed the "Pony Express" at Southern Methodist University, was a thoroughbred with the Rams from the get-go.

How so?

Dickerson won every award imaginable when he rushed for 3,913 yards in his first two years. That came on 769 carries.

That's a lot of rushes and maybe Rams coach John Robinson was channeling another former USC coach, John McKay, in giving Dickerson the football with regularity.

"What's the big deal?" McKay once quipped. "It doesn't weigh that much."

Yet Dickerson, the No. 2 pick in 1983, carried the weight of the Rams on his massive shoulder pads. Peeking from behind those intimidating goggles while gobbling up yardage, Dickerson led the NFL in rushing his first two years and in three of his four Rams seasons. He established an NFL single-season record when he rushed for 2,105 yards in his second year.

Despite a limited passing game during Dickerson's tenure, the offense featured plenty of giddy-up. As sure as there were horns on their helmets, the Rams were going to keep things on the down low.

"We were a running football team," Dickerson told Mighty 1090, a San Diego radio station. "That was our forte. It was our offense. It was identity.

When the "Pony Express" arrived from Southern Methodist University, he didn't disappoint. Dickerson was an All-Pro his rookie season and he followed that up with the greatest year ever by a running back. The future Pro Football Hall of Famer rushed for a single-season record 2,105 yards in 1984.

"Our identity was to run the football. You knew if we came to town our running game was going to be it. It could be third and seven or third and eight and we were going to run the football."

But certainly not at third and 33, right?

"I remember when we played the St. Louis Cardinals in St. Louis," Dickerson said. "It was third and 33 and we ran a toss play for 32 yards. That was just how we did it back then."

Those first two years helped catapult Dickerson to the game of his life in a 1985 playoff win over the Dallas Cowboys.

With Dieter Brock completing but 6 of 22 passes, it was pretty clear the Rams' attack started and ended with No. 29. They defeated the Cowboys, 20-0, as Dickerson rushed for an NFL postseason record 248 yards, with touchdown gallops of 55 and 40 yards.

A late-season performance of that caliber seemed improbable to a younger Dickerson.

"My first year in Week 11 or 12 if you look at the stats, man, my numbers dropped off," Dickerson said. "I dropped weight. I went from 225 to 212 and I was just tired.

"I won't forget when I came back to Texas in the offseason, I said I'm going to get ready for next year. Mentally and physically ready.

"When you come out of college you are used to playing a 12-game season, and in the pros you really have 20 games. Back then we played in the preseason. And then if you were fortunate enough you went into the playoffs. And if you are not accustomed to it, if your body isn't ready for it, it can be tough."

The NFL even brings the most invincible athletes to their knees.

"You don't expect it," Dickerson said. "A young guy doesn't expect to get run down."

The Game

By Eric Dickerson

I respect Dallas; they've always been a great football team, but I have never been a fan of Dallas. Some might think that's funny because I'm a native of Texas. But, as a kid, I always used to say that I'd love to play against the Dallas Cowboys.

Some people said that I had lost my desire and that I wasn't tough. But I love to play football and I give it my best every game.

I knew we could run at Dallas. You take away a team's strong point—Dallas' strong point is its team against the run—and you can win.

Dallas didn't think we could run on them. But our strength is our running game, and we knew we could run on them.

The first touchdown went for 55 yards to start the second half. It was a quick hit up the middle. For some reason, they were playing their safeties and cornerbacks up, maybe in a blitz. We knew if we could catch them in a blitz, we could burn them.

On the second scoring run in the fourth quarter, it was a pitch from Dieter Brock and I raced around the right side.

Michael Downs tried to tackle me high. There was no way I was going to let him tackle me.

It's been so long since I hit a home run—a long touchdown run. John Robinson has a way of making running backs feel invincible. After we busted the first play real good, you start to believe.

The previous two years, I didn't think we had a very strong team. But now I thought we did. I thought we could go all the way.

People say the running game is dead or gone. But it's the commitment that you make to it. Now you can't touch the receivers and you have to give them a cushion. Well of course you aren't going to run the football. But the teams that do run it are very dangerous.

And with the Rams, that's what we did: we ran the football. Our offense was built around running the football back in the 1980s. We knew we were going to run the football.

The Aftermath

Eric Dickerson's stint with the Rams didn't last much longer after the game of his life. When the two parties agreed to disagree regarding financial compensation, Dickerson was traded to the Indianapolis Colts two games into the 1987 season.

But Dickerson has long circled back to his original club and was among the Rams' biggest boosters since their return to Los Angeles.

"I just want my team to win," he says, when asked about the Rams.

Dickerson's winning ways paved his way to Canton, Ohio. The Pro Football Hall of Fame member got there with his hard-nose running, shifty moves, and a will that always had a way to shimmy from a tackle.

Dickerson, though, is insightful and gives credit elsewhere. While always confident about his abilities, he's also quick to share the glory.

As the second pick in 1983, Dickerson was the new kid on the block. The bigger kids doing the blocking were veterans.

"We had a seasoned offensive line," Dickerson said. "Jackie Slater gave me a stat, said, 'Eric, when you got to the Rams our offensive line had been together 6.5 years.'"

With age came precision. With snaps came the execution, which helped spring Dickerson on countless runs.

"Unless you have guys that come out of college and just mesh together, you have to have that experience up front," Dickerson said. "I don't care how big you are as a runner. I don't care how fast you are. I don't care how great you are. If you don't have the guys up front, you can't do it."

In 1983, from left to right, Dickerson's road pavers were Bill Bain, Kent Hill, Doug Smith, Dennis Harrah, and Slater. The next year, the only change was Slater being replaced by Irv Pankey. In 1985, Slater returned with Pankey flipping from right tackle to left tackle.

"The guys up front make us go," Dickerson said. "We make them look good at times, too. But they make us look extremely good, those guys up front. You depend on those guys."

Just like everyone leaned on Dickerson. Once Dickerson overhead teammate LeRoy Irvin talking up the Rams' powerful rushing game.

"When we had a 7- or 10-point lead with five or six minutes left in the game, we knew we had it," Irvin said.

"Because what are we going to do? We're going to run the football and you can't stop it."

That Dickerson's Rams career came to a premature halt still haunts Los Angeles fans. But Dickerson looks back with a smile and an atta-boy to his former protectors.

"You depend on those guys," he said. "I had a great appreciation and great admiration for my offensive linemen because that is a selfish job. They don't get a lot of praise for it, but we know what they are doing for us."

Chapter 16

KEVIN GREENE

Rams at 49ers—December 18, 1988

BIRTH DATE:	July 31, 1962
HOMETOWN:	Schenectady, New York
RESIDENCE:	Destin, Florida
JERSEY NO.:	91
POSITION:	Defensive end/linebacker
HEIGHT:	6 foot 3
WEIGHT:	245 pounds

The Run-Up

Kevin Greene's time at Auburn was well spent. The degree he earned in criminal justice proves it.

But as a football player? He was practically begging before the coaches finally let him play in his final two seasons.

Flash forward a few years, and Greene is in the NFL, and ultimately gets elected to the Pro Football Hall of Fame. Not bad.

As a football-loving youngster it dawned on Greene that he we would attend either the University of Alabama or Auburn University.

"I was born into an Alabama family," Greene said. "You're either Roll Tide or War Eagle. We grew up with [1971 Heisman Trophy winner] Pat Sullivan, when he was a player and coach at Auburn. And with my older brother Keith going to Auburn, there was no question where I was going to go."

Greene sent his prep game films to Auburn coaches and waited for his warm welcome. His patience, though, wasn't rewarded.

"They said they had given away all their scholarships," Greene said.

Auburn mentioned its coveted walk-on program and Greene bought in. But the dividends weren't much, as the 200-pound defensive end killed grass on the sidelines instead of tearing it up between the sidelines.

Greene quit and went into the school's ROTC program. He gained an edge by learning leadership skills and accumulated muscle by being a weight-room regular.

"I was 220 pounds now as a junior and I walked back on [the team]," Greene said. "It felt different this time. I had the eye of the tiger."

But he also caught glances from those who knew that Greene had yet to earn his stripes. Although he was older, he was treated as a newcomer.

"It was tough," Greene said. "Right out of the gate these big dudes were trying to kick my [tail] and the thing about it was they were very open about it. Players on that team would line up to take a repetition opposite me and they would yell, 'Kick his [tail] and send him back downtown.'

"That was the phase if they kicked someone's [tail] so bad that he would quit the team and you would send him downtown, because he didn't belong here. And they tried to do that to me."

What those delivering blows didn't know was that Greene had a plan to counter their brawn.

"It didn't take long to figure out that instead of absorbing the strike that was coming at you I found out by trying to meet that strike I could stop it. If they were coming to strike and I struck them harder, and not just meet them halfway, then they were going to go backward.

"If you can hit them harder than how they are hitting you is what it comes down to. I made up my mind that I was not going to let anyone out-hit me. I was going to kick their [tail]."

An exhausted but exhilarated Greene couldn't wait to share his excitement with his family. After practice he showed up with stories and his revered Auburn gear.

"I got my equipment—my Auburn Tiger helmet!—and brought it home," he said. "Everyone was saying, 'Put it on, put it on.' I said, 'No problem, I will sleep in this thing. Because this is what I have dreamed of.'

"Remember, this is just spring ball. I hadn't even made the team yet. But I was hitting with the big boys."

Greene soon would become a big man on campus. He started two years for Auburn, that rare junior walk-on who shows the game isn't too fast for him.

"I agree," said Greene, who was eventually inducted into the Alabama Sports Hall of Fame. "Not many players walk on as juniors."

Then again, not many had the drive and determination that Greene possessed. Those two traits led to him being selected by the Rams in the fifth round of the 1985 draft.

Being a late-round pick, Greene, much like he did at Auburn, had to prove his worth. He took his eye of the tiger to the pros, where he had a Pro Football Hall of Fame career in recording 160 sacks, third-best in NFL history and first among linebackers.

But only because he gave his best back when others doubted him.

"As a player, you just have to figure out the physical nature of the game," he said. "Either they are going to kick your [tail] or you are going to kick their [tail]. There is no in-between."

The Game

By Kevin Greene

It was the last game of the season in 1988, my fourth year in the league. We were playing the 49ers in Candlestick Park and we had to win this game to get into the playoffs. The 49ers had already qualified.

The Saturday night before the game I was watching "Rocky" on TV in the hotel room. I just remember Apollo Creed as he was dancing around Rocky and taunting Rocky. He was saying stuff like, "You can't hit me Rocky. I'm going to get you Rocky. You can't do this, you can't do that, Rocky."

Greene made football simple: if you hit harder than the other guy, you win. Greene was a winner with the Rams in what would be a Pro Football Hall of Fame career. Twice he had more than 16 sacks in a season for the Rams.

I remember jogging around the field the next day during warm-ups. I saw Joe Montana and Jerry Rice playing catch. I was watching Joe Montana warm up and I don't know where it came from but I was just so excited about playing against Joe Montana and everything that I went over to him and said, "I'm going to get you Joe, I'm going to get you Joe!"

Joe gave me a look like, "You idiot. What is your name? Do you even have a name?"

So I went on and had 4.5 sacks that game and four of the sacks came in the first quarter. We won the game, 38-16, and went to the playoffs.

I remember getting two sacks against Tom Rathman and he was a very good blocker, by the way. In my time in the NFL the best fullback I played against was Tom. But I got him a couple of times.

One of them might have come free and nobody hit me. I remember I beat the offensive tackle on another. I rolled outside and got up field on his shoulder. I was on him fast and I got to Montana. I was bringing it that game and it's as good [of] a game as I ever had.

I don't remember how the game went or if we were ever behind. I do remember that we won the game and we got into the playoffs that year. I just remember that was my biggest sack game of my career.

I had three sacks a few times and there were many, many games that I had two in a game.

But I never repeated having four-plus sacks in a game. And to do it in the last game of the regular season, against the Niners and Joe Montana, made it that more special.

That game came in my fourth year, but actually it was the first year that I was starting. The first three years I was primarily a special teams guy and designated third-down pass-rusher.

So I go into the starting role at outside linebacker and I end up being second in sacks to Reggie White. He had 18 and I was No. 2 with 16.5. And I still didn't make the Pro Bowl, which I thought . . . was odd.

The Aftermath

Kevin Greene got Joe Montana that day at Candlestick Park, and it's a story No. 91 relishes.

But it's also true that when you're a Hall of Famer, and a respectful player like Greene, you acknowledge Montana got him, too.

Greene's Rams stint was from 1985 to 1992, or what's referred to as the good old days in San Francisco, thanks to two Super Bowl titles during that span. With the 49ers playing at a level few teams could match, the Rams got a dose of Montana at least twice a year.

Super Joe was just that, and Greene picks at the Rams' losses to the Niners like stubborn scabs.

"With him being in our division we saw them every year," Greene said. "So I hunted him for three or four years as a starter and it was fun. I knew I was playing one of the best and my job was to get him."

One year after Greene was a pain to Montana, having sacked him four and a half times, revenge arrived.

The Rams were leading the 49ers, 24–10, going into the fourth quarter in a mid-December *Monday Night Football* game.

But Montana went Montana and rallied San Francisco for a 30–27 win. Montana had three touchdown passes, two of which went for more than 90 yards to John Taylor.

Weeks later in the NFC Championship Game, Montana tossed a pair of touchdown passes in leading San Francisco to a 30–3 victory. Super Joe had stopped the Rams from reaching their second Super Bowl.

In fact, the loss ended the Rams' final playoff run in Los Angeles. What followed was a series of dismal seasons before the team moved to St. Louis in 1995.

Greene and Montana had gone mobile as well. But their paths would cross as two savvy veterans seeking another championship. It was the 1993 AFC playoffs, with Greene still chasing Montana. Although this time Greene was with the Steelers and Montana with the Chiefs.

"That was my first year as a free agent after leaving the Rams," Greene said. "I was playing outside linebacker and we went to Kansas City to play Joe in a wild card game."

The game was, indeed, wild and ended in a predictable fashion for Greene. Montana's magic surfaced late as the Chiefs tied the game on his touchdown pass to Tim Barnett, and then won it in overtime, 27–24.

"Joe Montana beats us on [fourth down]," an exasperated Greene said. "He throws a touchdown pass to the back of the end zone and it could not have been a better throw or better timing."

Greene still can't believe Montana had time to get the pass off.

"I ended up leveling Joe just as the ball left his fingertips," Greene said. "I was going to make the play of the game. But just before I was going to knock the tar out of him and plant him into the ground he makes a throw to [tie] the game."

Once again, Montana got the upper hand, with a spent Greene sprawled on the turf.

"I'm laying on the ground on my back going, 'Oh my God, Joe Montana beat my [rear] all those years with the Rams and now he's with another team and he beat my [tail] again.'"

Greene was down but not out. A familiar face came over and made sure of just that. The player who once asked if Greene had a name extended a hand to a worthy foe.

"Joe put his hand down like you do for a handshake and he helped me up," Greene said.

Montana was brief.

"Great game, Greene," he said. "Just keep playing hard."

It's difficult for Greene to let that memory go. Especially now that Greene is a member of the Pro Football Hall of Fame with Montana.

"I always respected him for doing that," Greene said. "He knew that I was hunting him and he gave me a hand up after that last play. I was tortured out of my brain with him beating us again, but for him to help me up was an honor and I appreciated it."

Chapter 17

HENRY ELLARD

Colts at Rams—September 17, 1989

BIRTH DATE:	July 21, 1961
HOMETOWN:	Fresno, California
RESIDENCE:	San Antonio, Texas
JERSEY NO.:	80
POSITION:	Wide receiver/kick returner
HEIGHT:	5 foot 11
WEIGHT:	188 pounds

The Run-Up

Henry Ellard was more "Oh No" than "Oh Henry."

The flashy receiver landed with the Rams in 1983, a speedy second-round pick. But when he hit the unforgiving Giants Stadium turf his rookie year, it hit back.

"Broken collarbone," Ellard said. "I was out for five weeks. Nothing I could do but let it heal.

"I ran a skinny post up and over the top, a long pass, and I had to lay out for it. It's amazing how the mind works and you process that information in a split second. All this is going through my mind."

So he was making good on being something than the "other" pick the Rams made early in the 1983 draft. Ellard came into the NFL the same year as Eric Dickerson, so the shadows could easily find him.

"But I wanted to make an impression," Ellard said. "I went in the second round and Eric in the first round. Well, I wanted to show them what *I* can do."

"That first year, with the injury—I was second-guessing my whole career. I wasn't sure what was going to happen."

He healed, but had only 16 receptions to show for his rookie year.

When compared with Dickerson's first year—he rushed for 1,808 yards and 18 touchdowns—Ellard didn't do much.

But he didn't give up.

He leaned on his return skills to make his mark. While the Rams were content to hand Dickerson the ball, Ellard wanted to contribute beyond his position as a wide receiver.

"I just wanted to get his hands on the ball," he said.

Flying through the air with the greatest of ease was a breeze for Ellard. His ability to leap above defenders and catch the pass at its highest point made him a favorite among Rams quarterbacks. Ellard was a Pro Bowler at wide receiver and punt-returner. (AP Photo/Craig Fujii)

It was his quick feet that got him to the Pro Bowl as a punt-returner. His next two selections came as a wide receiver.

For that, Ellard still thanks Ernie Zampese.

The Rams were lost offensively after Eric Dickerson was traded to the Colts in 1987. Zampese arrived as an offensive coach in 1988 and Ellard couldn't believe what he was hearing from him.

"I remember sitting down and talking to him," Ellard said, "He said, 'You catch about 40–45 passes in a season, right? You can catch 70 balls in this system.' For me, that was hard to fathom."

The springy Ellard sprung to life in 1988, setting career highs in receptions (86), yards (1,414), and touchdown receptions (10).

"He made a believer out of me," Ellard said. "No doubt about it."

When three consecutive 1,000-yard seasons followed his first, Ellard's faith proved to be well-founded.

The Game

By Henry Ellard

I have so many fine memories from the game of football. But if you talk about a game where the numbers and everything just kind of stood out, I would have to go with the one in 1989 against the Indianapolis Colts.

I did my normal routine before the game. Nothing was different. Nothing out of the ordinary.

The funny part about it [was that it was] the first time Eric Dickerson came back to play in Anaheim after the Rams traded him. That was a big game because Eric was a good friend of mine.

But we really wanted to beat him *and* the Colts. And we did, 31–17.

It just so happens in this particular game I had 12 receptions for 230 yards and three touchdowns.

It was one of those days when everything just falls in place. We started catching them in the right coverages and started dialing it up. It was an exciting time, that's for sure.

Basketball players talk about being in the zone and for me it was just like that. Everything slowed down and it was amazing.

When I was running the routes, I was talking to myself—that slowed the game down for me. I'd think about running a certain route against a certain coverage, whether it was press coverage or not.

I would tell myself I had to stay on top of the route, to get the proper depth and be sharp breaking out the routes. I was thinking about all of that and it was like I was running in slow motion.

A lot of the catches I went up to get. I was a triple jumper, so it was natural for me.

They called me "Grasshopper" and shortened it down to "Hop."

If there was a high ball, I could go up and get it, that's for sure.

You have to know exactly what you are going to do when turning in the air for the ball.

When I had to go up and get it, it was always a challenge for me, especially going over the middle of the field. Because you knew the safety was bearing down on you, but you've got to make a catch.

I figured you know you're going to get hit. But it feels a whole lot better when you get up if the ball isn't laying on the ground.

They were playing zone that day, with the cornerback sitting probably 7 yards off the line of scrimmage, with some help right over the top.

I would come off the line and the cornerback starts backing up and that was close to utopia for me. I could take those little steps and turn inside and Jim [Everett] would throw it. I knew the ball was well on its way.

We came back and hit that again and again. With Ernie Zampese, and his background with Air Coryell, he knew if we caught them in the right coverage we could have a good game.

So we were running routine stuff and I was catching the ball and not getting tackled for 20 yards. Then we would come back and hit it again.

On one of the touchdowns the corner had outside leverage coverage and when I got the ball, he grabbed me and I spun out of the tackle. I kept on running until going into the end zone.

Another was on a skinny post where the corner was playing off. Jim had it there quickly. It was like playing catch with the quarterback. We kept pushing the corner back and it left the middle open and I would just turn in and go.

I wish I could remember the other one, but it's been so long ago. I know I would have had a fourth touchdown but a defender got a hand on the ball. It was pass interference and they didn't call it.

Still, it was an amazing day.

The Aftermath

Henry Ellard had an Olympic dream. After nine seasons in the NFL, he chased it.

"I was always a track guy," Ellard said. "Football was my first love, of course, but . . ."

Ellard was an exceptional triple jumper at Fresno State, setting the school mark by flying through the air with the greatest of ease.

Doing so was old hat for Ellard. He was piercing the sky at Fresno's Hoover High, where he won the state triple jump title.

But football called in 1983, which put his hopes of the 1984 Olympic Games on ice. He was going to Los Angeles, but as the Rams' second-round pick.

Fortunately for Ellard, by the time the 1992 Summer Games rolled around, the rules had been relaxed to allow professional athletes to compete. USA Basketball's Dream Team arrived and so did a thought bubble above Ellard's noggin.

"I started training for the Olympic Trials in the triple jump," Ellard said. "At that point I was really satisfied going into my 10th year [in the NFL], but I just wanted to try it. But I wasn't sure how I would do because it had been a while. It was like 10 years or so since I had attempted to jump."

Ellard competed in three meets.

"I decided I was going to do some jumping and see what happens," he said.

The bouncy Ellard, who went a school-record 55.05 feet at Fresno State, got some home cooking. His first meet was in Fresno, and with the locals fueling his fire, he jumped 52 feet.

"It had been a little while," he said. "I had to knock some rust off, that's for sure."

Next was the Mt. SAC Relays.

"I tried to jump and when I did, a shock went through my body," Ellard said. "I thought, 'Oh my God,' but it turned out to be a blessing."

A guardian angel came to Ellard's rescue, when it was clear he had the wrong shoes. Ray Kimble, one of Ellard's buddies, unlaced his cleats.

"He let me borrow his shoes," Ellard said. "He even showed me how to pad them a little to absorb the shock. If I could just get in a legal mark that day I could advance. I went 53 feet."

That sent Ellard to the Olympic Trials in New Orleans. Ellard, a bit amazed his dream still had oxygen, figured just to let the good times roll.

But much like the game of his life, the buzz going into the event was for someone else.

Eric Dickerson wasn't coming home, but decathlete Dan O'Brien was the big deal. O'Brien was part of a massive Nike marketing promotion leading up to the 1992 Summer Games.

Trouble was, O'Brien wasn't able to clear a single height in the pole vault and was eliminated.

It was time for Ellard to shine, and all systems were go.

"I felt pretty good," he said. "It was a nice day and it was a good runway."

And this time, Ellard wasn't running the risk of being shocked.

"I had my own shoes by that time," Ellard said with a laugh.

But a late misstep cost him. He fouled on his first jump and hoped the second one would be his charm.

Instead, the trail to the Crescent City hit a rough patch. Ellard's hamstring revolted on his second, and ultimately, last attempt.

"I never got a legal mark in," he said.

Just maybe he did something more important.

"I got to cross something off my bucket list, competing in the Olympic Trials," he said. "At least I tried and I have no regrets. It would have been something to make it but to have nine years in the [NFL] and still be doing the triple jump, I was ecstatic."

Chapter 18

JIM EVERETT

Rams at Buccaneers—December 6, 1992

BIRTH DATE:	January 3, 1963
HOMETOWN:	Emporia, Kansas
RESIDENCE:	San Clemente, California
JERSEY NO.:	11
POSITION:	Quarterback
HEIGHT:	6 foot 5
WEIGHT:	212 pounds

The Run-Up

Jim Everett had a problem in the 1986 draft, thanks to Houston.

"It all started when the Oilers had the No. 3 pick," Everett said.

NFL insiders thought Houston would select Alabama defensive end Jon Hand. With Warren Moon set at quarterback, the Oilers didn't need to strike by drafting another one with their first pick.

The Indianapolis Colts followed the Oilers on the draft board. Everett, a star at Purdue, was primed to stay in-state to begin his pro career.

"We were so sure that the Colts were going to pick me that my agent had a contract in place," Everett said. "I was going to come in from West Lafayette, show up the next day, have the contract ready to be signed, and then become a Colt.

"Then Houston got this grand idea right before the draft that they wanted Indianapolis fullback Randy McMillan. They said if you want Everett, we will switch spots for McMillan."

The Colts sniffed a bluff. Then the Oilers turned in their draft card: Everett.

"I hadn't talked to them and I didn't know anything about the Oilers," Everett said. "I didn't know who [coach] Jerry Glanville was. I had talked to Atlanta, I had talked to Indianapolis. But not Houston."

When Everett heard his name, he cringed like a Texas wildcatter finding another dry hole. He really turned sour when he learned the Oilers were going to pay him half of what he had agreed to with the Colts. This, despite being drafted one spot higher by Houston.

"And they laced it with incentives that if I was riding the pine behind Warren Moon, they wouldn't have to pay me," Everett said. "I said, 'Wait a minute. If the Colts are offering me "X" and you are offering me half of that, well . . .'" I was always going to be trade bait. They never intended to bring me in."

Training camp came and went with Everett in a stalemate with the Oilers.

Finally, just before the trade deadline, talks heated up. The Colts remained interested, but it was 49ers quarterback Joe Montana's health that led to Everett being traded to the NFC West-rival Rams.

"I ended up with the Rams, basically, because of Joe Montana's bad back," Everett said. "The Rams didn't want me playing for San Francisco. But for a while I thought I was going to Green Bay. [Packers coach] Forrest Gregg called me on Monday to say he was trying to get me to Green Bay by Thursday so I could start on Monday night against the Bears.

"The Bears in 1986? They were just coming off their Super Bowl win. I said, 'You got to be [kidding] me.'"

Instead the Rams shipped All-Pro guard Kent Hill, future Pro Bowl defensive end William Fuller, and three draft picks, two being first-rounders, to the Oilers for Everett's big right arm.

"We paid full price," Rams coach John Robinson said. "We weren't looking for a bargain. But we made a dynamic move to be a major factor in the NFL for years to come."

Everett would deliver just that, becoming the most prolific passer in Rams history by throwing for 23,758 yards. But he's on the Rams' summit only after a wild stint in which he was the Oilers' property, and being pursued by the Colts, 49ers, Packers, and Rams.

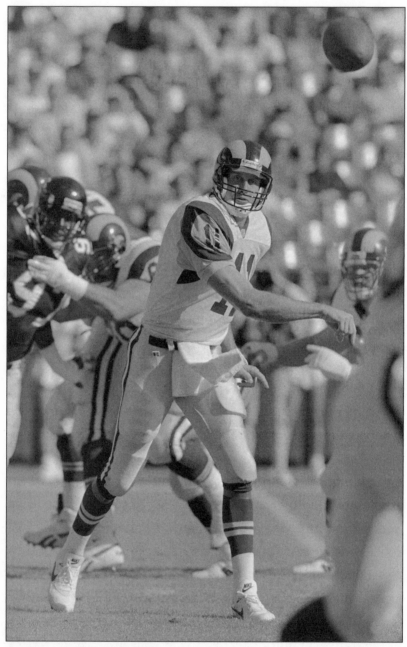

Everett fell short in his quest to get the Rams to the Super Bowl but he left behind some staggering statistics. His 23,758 passing yards are the most in franchise history and his 142 touchdown passes are second only to Roman Gabriel's total of 154 among Rams. (AP Photo)

"I went to bed with four different helmets on four different nights," Everett said.

He settled for the one with horns on it.

The Game

By Jim Everett

You go through your schedule when it comes out and look at some games as [either a] definite win or as a tough game. Everybody does that as you try to figure out which ones you think you'll win and where you're going to sneak out a tough game.

The Tampa Bay game was one on the book that you chalk up for a win. They weren't outstanding at the time; not that we were super-strong either. But we expected to win that one.

Then the game starts and we're doing nothing and then we do more of nothing. Turnovers . . . we just stunk up the place in the first half. It was not good football for us on either side of the ball and we go down 27–3.

I remember at halftime there were a lot of emotions flying around. It wasn't the finger-pointing emotion, it was more what's happening against a bad team? Who the heck are we to be down by 24 points to a team like this?

No matter what sport you are playing you have to do more than just show up and basically we just showed up. We weren't playing anything close to Rams football.

Sure, the Buccaneers had some things go their way, but still.

So we come out in the second half and it was time to get into the end zone with some strikes. They are playing Cover 2 coverage. With the Cover 2 you want to stretch someone down the middle to open up the guys on the outside and put the pressure on the safeties. But it takes time for that to happen and we had little protection in the first half.

It's a kind of bend-but-don't-break coverage. But you can break it if you get enough protection.

We needed a spark, so we send two guys down the middle over the linebackers and [Willie] Flipper [Anderson] is on the outside. I immediately hit him for a 40-yard touchdown to pull us within 27–10.

Our defense started to feed off us and as a team, we just never stopped believing. It would have been easy for us to say it's just a bad day and just let this game go. But that's not what sports are all about and it was proven when watching the last Super Bowl [LI]. Even though the Patriots were down by 25 points, they were never out of it because they believed.

That's the mentality that you have to have. And you need to get lucky a little bit.

If you have the tenacity and will power—and you've got some quarters left and overtime—you got a chance. Whoever said it ain't over until the fat lady sings, well that's been repeated many times.

So we get it started with Flipper, and God bless him because we were zipping it around and I was connecting with him.

Jeff Chadwick scored the next touchdown on a 27-yard pass to make it 27–17.

Then David Lang scores from the 1-yard line late in the third quarter, although I know it was passing plays that got us down there. Lang was a late-round draft pick and was talented. Plus, he was a really funny dude. Now the score is 27–24.

The final touchdown, in the fourth quarter, went to Pat Carter from 8 yards out to put us ahead, 31–27.

I remember him catching that ball and I'll never forget that smile; it's amazing the little things you remember. I remember his smile. When he turned around it was the most magnetic smile. I don't recall anything fabulous about the catch or the throw, but I do remember that smile.

It was amazing because if you think about it from within two hours of time, it was like going from the morgue to a wedding reception. It was that type of a roller coaster.

Basically, that's what makes fans so interested in the NFL. It's what gets the players ready to play the next week. It's those types of feeling you miss when you're not playing. It's defying those highs and lows, from where you go from being the world's worst team to being on fire. And we were on fire in that second half. It was a great way to end the day.

It's like we were champions for that day. It was one of those kinds of moments.

When I give my motivational talks to my kids, that's the game I always refer to.

The Aftermath

The Rams were overhauling their roster, which meant Jim Everett was inquiring about U-Hauls.

"Everyone likes to be loved, we really do," Everett said.

But Everett and the Rams had lost that loving feeling.

After the Rams lost seven of their first 10 games with Everett under center in 1993, coach Chuck Knox pointed him to the bench.

From the game of his life to splinters in his backside, that was how Everett's illustrious Rams tenure tapered out.

But like that day when he rallied the Rams over Tampa Bay, Everett never relinquished hope.

After his ups and downs with the Rams, Everett was traded to the New Orleans Saints in 1994.

"God bless Chuck Knox, but I wasn't the quarterback for what they wanted to do," Everett said. "When they talk about revamping the offensive line, revamping the receivers, and they're in the middle of that process and you're the quarterback? Well, it [stinks]."

But Saints coach Jim Mora smelled a rose where the Rams pinched their nose. Mora's affection for Everett was linked to 1989, when Everett threw for 454 yards in leading the Rams to an amazing comeback overtime victory in New Orleans.

"I needed a new venue, and going to New Orleans really brought some new life to me," Everett said. "I don't want to be negative, but the atmosphere with the Rams then was a little negative and I didn't want to be part of it.

"New Orleans hadn't had a lot of throwers. Most of their quarterbacks had been game managers. They had some guys with talent, they just weren't able to whip the ball around the park like we did against the Saints in that comeback win. I think Mora was intrigued with that, and that game was part of it. I really believe that.

"I came in and we got in the top 10 of offense and it was really fun. The defense was falling down a little but it was still fun."

Everett landed in New Orleans because Henry Ellard was out that historic day against the Saints, when Willie "Flipper" Anderson had an NFL-high 336 receiving yards.

"Ellard is down with a hamstring so we had to move some players around," Everett said. "Willie was playing 'Z' receiver and we moved him over to the 'X' spot. Then we put Aaron Cox out to replace Anderson.

"That was a big deal and I was worried. Ellard was my security blanket. He was the one I could throw to coming out of the break, the one I had the timing down with so well. I was a little nervous without him out there."

Everett had an interesting view that day of the Superdome. Too many times he looked at its ceiling, prone on his back.

"The first half I got sacked six or seven times," he said. "It's hard to hold on to the ball with Pat Swilling and Rickey Jackson coming at you. But we came back to win the game, even though we were still down by 14 points with four minutes left."

Those turning away prematurely missed a heck of a rally.

"It was the Sunday night game and we could virtually hear all the TV sets across the country being clicked off," Everett said. "Then it was boom, boom, and Flipper is catching everything I throw his way. He was the best player on the planet that night. I tell you what, I wasn't looking at Cox. With Flipper on fire, I stayed right there."

It was a performance that helped put Everett in New Orleans five years later. He spent three years in the Bayou, before ending his career in 1997 with the San Diego Chargers.

He exited America's Finest City with the team's finest regular-season, win-loss mark for a starting quarterback: 1–0.

While Everett made his mark with the Rams, he came into the NFL as an Oiler and went out as a winner.

Chapter 19

KURT WARNER

Rams vs. Titans—January 30, 2000

BIRTH DATE:	June 21, 1971
HOMETOWN:	Burlington, Iowa
RESIDENCE:	Scottsdale, Arizona
JERSEY NO.:	13
POSITION:	Quarterback
HEIGHT:	6 foot 2
WEIGHT:	214 pounds

The Run-Up

Kurt Warner was showing off his right arm, the one that would eventually transform him into a Super Bowl-winning quarterback and a two-time NFL MVP.

But he wasn't connecting with targets in front of scouts. He wasn't doing it in front of a stadium full of fans.

Instead, the venue for Warner to keep his accuracy sharp was the Hy-Vee store in Cedar Falls, Iowa.

Before the dawn's early light, Warner was picking off co-workers from afar in 1994.

"I remember breaking open bags of candy and gummy bears," Warner said. "The game was to kind of see where the other people were stocking shelves. Then you would try to throw it over the top of the shelves and hit them."

Warner's trek to the game of his life is like no other.

He was the University of Northern Iowa's third-string quarterback until his senior year. After a solid season, he was thought of well enough to get an invitation to the Green Bay Packers' 1994 training camp as an undrafted rookie.

But he was cut and he moved back to Iowa. Warner was hired, at $5.50 an hour, to stock shelves at the Hy-Vee.

"We would be in the break room and everyone would always ask each other what they were going to do in the future," Warner said. "I would tell everyone that I was going to play in the NFL and win the Super Bowl."

Warner had a strong arm and a keen knack for visualizing a future few others saw. He recalls working the cereal aisle where boxes of Sugar Pops, Rice Krispies, and Life would battle for the customers' attention.

But there was one brand that connected with Warner over the others.

"I would stock the Wheaties and they would have all these great athletes on the boxes," he said. "And I thought, 'One day I'm going to be on a Wheaties box.' And it was amazing that that came true, too.

"There are so many different stories from that time that a lot of people don't know about. But I think back on those days quite often."

From hanging at the Hy-Vee, Warner joined the Arena League. It was there his game blossomed and soon after he would emerge from the dark shadows of anonymity.

He played two years with the Iowa Barnstormers, taking them to the Arena Bowl in both seasons. He was granted a tryout with the Chicago Bears before his second year with Iowa, in 1997. But he was bitten by a spider in his right elbow during his honeymoon and was unable to throw.

The St. Louis Rams acquired him in 1998, but he was far from a finished project. They allocated him to NFL Europe's Amsterdam Admirals, where he paced the league in touchdown passes and passing yards.

Warner exited Europe and became the Rams' third-string quarterback that same year. He completed a whopping four passes.

A Rams quarterback shuffle in 1999 ended with Warner becoming Trent Green's backup. But in an exhibition game that summer, Chargers safety Rodney Harrison dove at Green's legs on a safety blitz and demolished Green's left knee in the process.

The Rams thought their season was in shambles as well. But Warner threw for a league-high 41 touchdowns and 4,353 yards.

From a clerk at a market to being the Super Bowl XXXIV MVP, few players can match Warner's amazing story. The only shocker was that his dramatic, storybook season—he was also the NFL MVP—came when the team played in St. Louis, and not closer to Hollywood.

The "Greatest Show on Turf" was born, and for an NFL-record three straight seasons the Rams scored at least 500 points.

Of course that 1999 season ended with Warner's game of his life, when he directed the Rams to their first and only Super Bowl victory.

"It's funny that after I did it those people at the Hy-Vee already knew I could do it," Warner said. "Because I was pretty good at throwing those gummy bears."

The Game

By Kurt Warner

How can it get any better than Super Bowl XXXIV? To come out and get the opportunity to throw for 400 yards in a Super Bowl, in your first Super Bowl, and set a record there and win the championship.

How it played out was so special after the Titans tied it up, 16–16, with about two minutes left.

I just remember being on the sidelines and coach [Dick] Vermeil saying, "You've always dreamed of this." Just think of how many times you've thought about directing the game-winning drive and then throw the game-winning pass in the Super Bowl.

For me the 73-yard touchdown pass to Isaac Bruce couldn't have been more fitting. He was in L.A. when we made the move to St. Louis and he was one of few significant guys that was still with the team.

Even though he hadn't had much success that year, every day in practice he was a model of excellence, of how to compete, and how to play the game. Everyone else just followed his lead.

So it was fitting that he was the guy that made the play for us. For much of the year Marshall Faulk was the story for us with it being his first year in St. Louis.

But [Bruce] was the Ram that really set the tone for us. And he was the guy that made the offensive play of the Super Bowl for us.

We hadn't thrown that route the entire game. The play was "Twins Right Ace Right 999." We had used it throughout the season and we talked about it all week that if we got man-to-man coverage on the corners. Then they went with that coverage.

It was a go route for Isaac and it was something we talked about throwing on his back shoulder. If I could lay it up there perfectly on the outside, the safety wouldn't be in position to challenge it.

I got hit by Jevon Kearse when I threw it and from the force of that [hit] the pass was little bit short. But Isaac turned around to make the catch and with Az-Zahir Hakim making the key block; so many different factors go into that one play.

But after Isaac's catch that put us ahead, 23–16, all we could do was to go stand on the sidelines. We just had to wait to see how it all played out.

One of the hardest things about football is you only play one way and that is what makes it the ultimate team sport. When I could get the ball back in my hands, I would feel more comfortable. From our standpoint, we had done what we had to do and now we had to put our trust to the guys on the field. The defense had to do its part.

Everyone saw our team as "The Greatest Show on Turf." But the defense was forgotten and it had made so many huge plays for us that year. I don't think people gave our defense as much credit as it deserved. And it made the big play for us that really finished it off. We complemented each other so well.

We were sitting there watching the game's last play [from the Rams' 10-yard line] and we knew [Titans quarterback Steve] McNair didn't throw it in the end zone. So that was a plus. We saw that it was a completion and then Mike [Jones] made the tackle. But we couldn't tell if [Kevin Dyson] had made it into the end zone.

So everyone is looking up at the scoreboard, looking at the zeros up there, and then looking to see where the officials were.

Were they going to signal a touchdown or wave it off?

Obviously when they waved it off, that Dyson didn't score, it was clear that I had had a magical season in my first season as a starter.

That game was the culmination of so many different things. I was thinking back, just about the process and the journey. And then for it to finish that way in my first year as starter was really something.

It was one of those magical games and it was the end to a magical season. I don't think we could have written it better or could have dreamed it as well as it played out. It was pretty incredible.

We had come in very confident that they couldn't stop us. And they couldn't, other than the fact that we couldn't finish and put more points on the board. I overthrew Ricky Proehl at the end of the half on what might had been a touchdown, and earlier I had a fumbled snap. We really dominated the first half, but we allowed them to stay in the game. It was only 9–0 at the half.

Sometimes you wish you could blow the other team out. But there is nothing better than to play in a Super Bowl and make the critical play down the stretch to seal the game.

So it ended the way it was supposed to end, the way I had dreamed of.

The Aftermath

Fairy tales require special endings. So how could Kurt Warner's finish in any other fashion?

Warner, a rags-to-riches story, had a nifty final chapter.

"My journey is unlike anybody else's," he said.

Warner's game of his life led to him getting the game's loftiest honor. The Pro Football Hall of Fame made room for the former Hy-Vee clerk in its aisle of 2017 inductees.

The quarterback who once couldn't find a team was chosen to be among the NFL's most hallowed squad.

"It might not define me, but it adds to the definition," Warner said. "And I kind of like that."

With Canton, Ohio, calling, Warner became the 30th Ram to make the Hall of Fame. Of those, 18 played a significant portion of their careers with the Rams.

Warner's presence did wonders for the Rams, the team that gave him that chance he longed for.

But his impact wasn't just felt by the Rams.

Warner spent the 2004 season with the New York Giants, where he mentored a hot-shot rookie from Ole Miss: Eli Manning.

With Manning starting right away, Warner looked elsewhere for an opportunity.

Warner rose again in the Valley of the Sun in 2005, taking the Arizona Cardinals to destinations they only dreamed of.

"A lot of people thought I couldn't do it anymore," Warner said. "They said I was starting to show my age."

But with the years came wisdom. The Cards hitched their hopes to Warner and he led the way.

The zenith was the 2008 season when the Cardinals, after winning a division title for the first time since 1975, advanced to their first Super Bowl. Warner threw for more than 300 yards in his third Super Bowl. But it was in a losing cause, as the Pittsburgh Steelers won, 27–23.

Warner's long and winding road was coming to an end. But not before his final season in 2009 produced another postseason appearance, once more coming with a sprinkling of Warner magic.

Arizona opened the playoffs by beating the Green Bay Packers in overtime, 51-45. Warner, sensing it was his last home game, put on a show. He had more touchdown passes [five] than incompletions [four].

"It was one of those special games," said Warner, only the second NFL player to throw for 100 touchdown passes for two teams, the Rams and Cardinals. "It felt like I was going to make every throw.

"I knew I was probably retiring and I wanted the fans in the new stadium [for the Cardinals] to remember me."

Warner left good impressions no matter where he hung his shoulder pads. An inspiration because of his resolve and the manner in which he carried himself, Warner contributed to teams in ways that aren't revealed with statistics.

"Going back to the Rams, there were a lot of ups and downs," Warner admitted. "I had bounced around to a lot of different teams."

But he'll change no more. The Hall of Fame is that rare team where no one gets released or traded.

"The way my journey played out, starting my first NFL game at 28, having some bumps along the way in a couple of organizations, I don't know if I ever really felt I did enough [to make the Hall]," Warner said. "When I was between the lines, I felt like I played this game as well as anybody. Is that enough to get there? I have no idea."

We do. The proof is a gold Hall of Fame jacket for someone once wearing a store clerk's apron.

Chapter 20

JOHNNY HEKKER

Seahawks at Rams—October 19, 2014

BIRTH DATE:	February 8, 1990
HOMETOWN:	Redmond, Washington
RESIDENCE:	Los Angeles, California
JERSEY NO.:	6
POSITION:	Punter
HEIGHT:	6 foot 5
WEIGHT:	225 pounds

The Run-Up

If Johnny Hekker was going to be a busy Beaver, he would do so as Oregon State's quarterback; or at least that was his intention.

"That was always a little bit in the back of my mind," he said. "I would start off as a punter and end up in the quarterbacks' room."

Nevertheless, it was Hekker's right leg that intrigued Oregon State coach Mike Riley. But Hekker's right arm had plenty of kick, too.

Hekker led Bothell (Washington) High to the 4A state finals his senior year by taking snaps. He threw for 55 touchdowns and collected nearly 2,000 passing yards in just 14 games.

So it was no passing fancy that Hekker, a prep star in three other sports, thought he could heave the football at the college level.

But Hekker could read a depth chart. He took inventory of the Beavers' roster and saw a half dozen quarterbacks and zero punters.

Trouble was Riley had the same number of punters as he did scholarships for punters—zero. The former Chargers coach did promise Hekker good things if he took a leap of faith with the Beavers.

"So I walked on, went to Corvallis, [Oregon], and loved the whole thing," said Hekker, who eventually got a scholarship.

The love came back in 2010 when Hekker boomed a 74-yard punt against USC.

But few were saying "cheese" versus Wisconsin when Hekker shanked a negative-4-yard punt.

That's the life of a quarterback-turned-punter, and at least Hekker never kicked away his scholarship.

What he did toss was his dream of taking snaps.

"It just never materialized and I ended up being pleased with that," he said. "I just really enjoyed becoming a specialist and trying to master my craft, my punting. I also realized if you're a quarterback, you didn't really have a lot of other free time to focus on other things. I really didn't miss it."

Unfortunately for Hekker, he did miss out on being selected in the 2012 draft.

"I believed I was going to be drafted, but that didn't happen," he said. "But in the long run I got to choose my team, and I chose the Rams. They had told me they wanted me to be their guy and that they had confidence in me.

"And getting to be in the NFC West, we would play Seattle every year. I could try to beat the team that I grew up watching, that was my attitude."

So Hekker rolled the dice again, similar to his situation with Oregon State.

"It was a great fit, but I really wasn't too sure what to expect," Hekker said. "NFL punters are really consistent and I wasn't quite there yet. I knew that and I knew I really had to work really hard to improve."

John Fassel, then the Rams' special teams coach, took an interest in Hekker. Their personalities clicked and Hekker didn't disappoint Fassel.

"With Coach Fassel's guidance I was able to continue to get better, hang around, and stick with the team," Hekker said. "The Rams believed in my game and also how hard I was willing to work."

Hekker's right leg was his ticket to Oregon State and the Rams. But he needed both legs, otherwise he wouldn't have been able to walk on at both levels.

Weapons can be found all over the field and Hekker is one for the Rams. With his strong and accurate leg, Hekker can flip the field position quickly. A two-time Pro Bowler, Hekker has helped change how punters contribute to a team. After making the team as an undrafted rookie, he's been selected to three Pro Bowls.

The Game

By Johnny Hekker

I would probably say the 28–26 win at home in St. Louis when I threw a pass off a fake punt against Seattle at the end of the game. I was able to hit Benny Cunningham on a little out route.

That was the game where we had a lot of plays from the special teams. That allowed us to get the win for us. I don't think the offense scored a touchdown.

Stedman Bailey returned a punt 90 yards for a touchdown on a tricky return. It was either going to work well or we were going to look foolish for even trying it. . . . It was a play we had seen, and you see Jon Ryan's punt chart, and 99.9 percent of his balls are going to the same spot, so we said, "You know, let's give this thing a shot," and our guys executed well.

On my pass to Cunningham, it was late in the fourth quarter and our drive had stalled at our 18-yard line. Seattle was kind of rolling, so we didn't want to give the ball back to them. It was just at that part of a game where Seattle was taking the momentum back, you could feel it.

So Coach [Jeff] Fisher and special-teams coach [Jim] Fassel, well we had a play drawn up. No matter what, we were going to run the play and try not to give the ball back to Seattle.

It's very fun for that to happen, but it's also, to whom much is given, much is expected, so we've got to make sure we're always ready and do our best when we do have those fake opportunities just to make sure we know what we're doing. We practice it enough that we are ready to go on Sundays.

Being able to play for a coach that does like to throw that kind of stuff in quite frequently is kind of fun. Throwing the players a bone who sometimes don't get recognized gives them a little bit of an opportunity to get some attention out there.

I was able to connect with Benny Cunningham as he came out in the flat off the left wing. He was such a good athlete that all I had to do was get the ball to him and let him run with it.

We ran a guy out in kind of a misdirection, which let Benny come out in the flat. That created some confusion with their man-to-man coverage. We knew he would be open if we executed the play right. When knew if we sent a guy in motion, a Seattle defender would go with him, and he did. It was great.

I threw Benny a good pass and he turned it up field for 10 yards and we ended up running out the clock. That was the last possession.

It was so big because we couldn't give them the ball back. [Seahawks quarterback] Russell Wilson was heating up and our defense, which had played well, was tired.

It was just a moment when we knew we had to keep the ball if we wanted to win. So we took a shot and it paid off with us hitting the pass.

It's funny, but I actually didn't get the call when we were taking the field; no one said anything to me. Then some guys run by me and I hear the play call and I thought it was a joke at first. Then I'm like, "Holy cow, here we go."

It was the kind of thing where I'm glad I didn't have too much time to really think about it. It ended up working out, it was a great call by Coach Fisher.

It was a play we had run a ton in practice and just had yet to get the look in the game. We had the right look and we were able to run it to perfection.

So I get back 15 yards from the ball and my heart starts beating faster than normal. It was just a great moment.

I knew Benny was a good enough athlete that he could make the catch and do something with it.

The pass was a pretty tight spiral. I would rate it a seven out of a 10. I remember I took my time with it and I stepped into the pass. It was a confident throw and he had enough time to turn it up field.

Come to think of it, it was a perfect pass. The tightest spiral ever—ha!

We had practiced it so many times and we were so waiting for the moment to call it. That was the first time we used it that season and it was the only time we used that play the whole season.

Once you show it, then it gets on film and the [rival] special-teams coaches will be looking for that motion, which tells them that the play is coming.

We didn't use it again. But it's nice to make the other special-teams coaches stay up a little longer at night preparing for it. It gives them something else to worry about.

That is another thing plays like that do. You want to make it difficult for other teams to prepare for you.

Because you never know. They have to account for the matchups, just in case we use that play again.

The Aftermath

Johnny Hekker, a difference-maker? That's seldom said about NFL punters.

What's rarer is Patriots coach Bill Belichick raving about a punter not his own.

"Hekker is a tremendous weapon," Belichick said before the Rams-Patriots game in 2016. "I mean, this guy is as good a player as I've ever seen at that position.

"He's a tremendous weapon in his ability to punt the ball, punt it inside the 20, directional kick it, involved in fakes, can throw, can run, very athletic.

"He's dangerous. Absolutely. He's like a quarterback. He can throw. He can run. You gotta defend him like you defend one of those guys."

That's high praise to a degree that it makes Hekker's complexion match his red hair.

A tad embarrassing, but who's to argue with the coach who's won five Super Bowls?

"That's pretty cool," Hekker said. "And pretty incredible.

"At first I didn't know if he was taking a shot at the Rams by talking about me; we weren't doing that great at the time. But he was sincere and for it to come from a proven winner like that is the ultimate compliment."

Hekker, a three-time All Pro, has grown since the game of his life. But Belichick's comments also serve as a reflection of the well-rounded Hekker's game. While his punting was key, so was his passing that day against the Seattle Seahawks in the game of his life.

In essence, there's more ways to contribute as a punter than many think. With Hekker, that translates into precision efforts, where he places the football exactly where he planned. Winning the field-position game can never be overemphasized.

"There's more to it than just hitting a spiral down the middle of the field," Hekker said. "You can do directional punts, pooch punts, fakes, put people in motion."

Punters and kickers have always been looked at differently by their teammates. It's the nature of an occupation where you're specialized to do one thing and one thing only.

But the thing with Hekker is he's such an accomplished athlete that his body does things that many other punters can't.

"Teams are looking for punters now that have a skill-set that can do more than just punt," Hekker said. "I think punters have really taken a step forward."

When Hekker steps back to his football roots, his leadership skills are close to the surface. The former star prep quarterback remains vocal on the field, and if people will follow a punter into action, so be it.

"I know that you are much less involved in the grand scheme of things, the game-planning and stuff, to be that guy," Hekker said. "But if I can bring that energy to the punts and the field-goal teams and the special-teams players . . . if I can help raise their level of completion by showing some encouragement and just my love of the game, that is the beauty of it.

"I don't really think about being a leader, but maybe I am by being true to myself and showing how blessed we are to play this game."

Hekker still awaits the biggest kick of his life. It'll come when the Rams win a Super Bowl and share it with a Southern California fan base that has welcomed them back to their Los Angeles home.

"I envision it all the time," Hekker said. "Just what it would be like to hoist that Vince Lombardi Trophy as a team and with the Rams' horns on our helmets.

"But I know that it is not just going to happen because you wish it would or that you visualized that it would. It takes action and hard work."

That's something one of Hekker's super fans, Bill Belichick, knows all about.